T0039936

FIVE MINUTES
of
GRACE

FIVE MINUTES

of

GRACE

DAILY DEVOTIONS

365 Inspirations to Encourage Your Soul
Every Day of the Year

Written by Tama Fortner

HOWARD BOOKS

ATRIA

NEW YORK   LONDON   TORONTO   SYDNEY   NEW DELHI

An Imprint of Simon & Schuster, Inc.
1230 Avenue of the Americas
New York, NY 10020

First Howard Books hardcover edition November 2020

HOWARD BOOKS/**ATRIA** B O O K S and colophons are
trademarks of Simon & Schuster, Inc.

For information about special discounts for bulk purchases,
please contact Simon & Schuster Special Sales at
1-866-506-1949 or business@simonandschuster.com.

The Simon & Schuster Speakers Bureau can bring authors
to your live event. For more information or to book an event,
contact the Simon & Schuster Speakers Bureau at
1-866-248-3049 or visit our website at www.simonspeakers.com.

Interior design by Davina Mock

Manufactured in the United States of America

3 5 7 9 10 8 6 4 2

Library of Congress Cataloging-in-Publication Data
has been applied for.

ISBN 978-1-9821-3301-6
ISBN 978-1-9821-3302-3 (ebook)

The law works fear and wrath; grace works hope and mercy.

—Martin Luther

JANUARY

Grace

It is by grace you have been saved, through faith . . .
<small>EPHESIANS 2:8 NIV</small>

In the Hebrew of the Old Testament, the word for "grace" is חֵן (*chen*); in the Greek of the New Testament, it is χάρις (*charis*). In either language the meaning is largely the same: *the favor of the Lord.* It's a word that whispers gratitude, kindness, and graciousness, something both wondrously pleasant and precious. It is *unmerited favor*, many scholars say.

Defining "grace" across the Bible in Hebrew and Greek can seem complex, but grace itself isn't complicated. Not really. For all the scholarly definitions that can be found and studied, perhaps the best definition is also the simplest: Grace is the unending goodness of God poured out on His oh-so-undeserving people.

Today, look for ways to embrace His grace in your life.

Holy Father, sometimes my prayers become complicated with my own attempts to figure everything out. But, like grace, prayer isn't complicated. Not really. It's simply a way to speak to You—to say thank You. And I do, Lord. I thank You so very much. Amen.

Give and Be Given

"Give, and it will be given to you. A good measure,
pressed down, shaken together and running
over, will be poured into your lap. For with the
measure you use, it will be measured to you."

LUKE 6:38 NIV

Luke 6:38 promises us something beautiful: *Give, and it will be given to you.* How many stories have you heard of people who have given their money to the Lord and then had Him return it in the most unexpected of ways?

But what if this promise applies to something other than just money and things? What if it is true for faith, trust, love, and grace? If you give your faith and trust to God, will He not strengthen that faith and help you trust Him even more? Give your love away to Him and to others, and just see how much more love you receive in return. Give your grace to those who have need of it, and God will give you His grace . . . pressed down, shaken together, and running over.

What can you give away today?

*Lord, teach me not to ration the faith, the trust, the
love, and the grace that I give away. Because I know
You do not ration all that You give to me. Amen.*

While We Were Still Sinners

But God demonstrates his own love for us in this:
While we were still sinners, Christ died for us.

ROMANS 5:8 NIV

While we were still sinners. Is there any more powerful statement of love than this? While we were still ignoring God and choosing our own paths. While we were still flinging our rebellion up at Him like a toddler throwing a tantrum over a toy. While we were knowingly doing the very things He asked us not to do.

That is when God sent Jesus.

Sin makes an enemy of God, and so our sins should have made us enemies of God. They should have earned punishment and His eternal wrath. Instead, He gave us grace. Simply because He loves us, deeply and entirely.

*Lord, words are not enough to thank
You for the grace You give me while
I am still a sinner. Amen.*

Of Course Not!

Well then, since God's grace has set us free from the law,
does that mean we can go on sinning? Of course not!

ROMANS 6:15 NLT

I f God's going to forgive me anyway for the bad things that
I do, or the ways in which I do not love my neighbor, isn't it
okay to keep acting the way I've always acted? In Paul's own
words: "Of course not!"

God's grace does not free us from the obligation to obey
Him. Jesus Himself said, "If you love me, keep my commands"
(John 14:15 NIV). Rather, God's grace frees us from the penalty
of our sins. Our sins have earned us a death sentence, but
God's grace has voided that sentence. His grace covers our sins
with the righteousness of Christ and offers us eternal life in
heaven instead.

Today, when you are tempted to act in a way you know
would not please God, remember His grace—and in your freedom, choose not to sin.

Dear Lord, let me never take Your grace for
granted. Help me to obey You in all things
simply because I am grateful. Amen.

Before Time Began

God saved us and chose us to be his holy people.
We did nothing to deserve this, but God planned it
because he is so kind. Even before time began God
planned for Christ Jesus to show kindness to us.

2 TIMOTHY 1:9 CEV

Before light filled the skies . . . before the first ocean wave rippled upon the shore. . . before that first forbidden fruit was ever plucked from the tree . . . from the very start—*that's* when God first planned to send His Son to live on earth and die to save us.

Imagine that. As God called forth the sun, moon, and stars; as He scooped up the dust and breathed life into man; as He walked with Adam and Eve in the cool of the garden, He knew they—*we*—would turn away from Him. But instead of walking away, He made a plan to sacrifice His only Son—Himself—for us.

Right from the very start . . . before time began.

O Lord, You know my every mistake, my every sin—You've always known them, from before I was even born. You've always known how much I need Jesus. Please help me to know that too and to see evidence of your kindness today. Amen.

The Lord Is Just

"The Lord is just! He is my rock! There is no evil in him!"
PSALM 92:15 NLT

What does it mean when the Bible says our Lord is just? He is upright, correct, and pleasing. There is no crookedness or evil in Him. We can trust completely, and without reservation, in His goodness—and we can know that He will carry out justice.

God is also straightforward: He does not hide Himself from us. If you seek Him in His Word, His message is clear: Jesus said, "I am the way and the truth and the life. No one comes to the Father except through me" (John 14:6 NIV). Like a rock, God's truth never changes—and neither does He.

You can build your life on the justness of God—starting today.

Lord, You are my Rock—just, righteous,
and unchanging in Your truths. Help me,
Lord, to build my life on You. Amen.

The Gift of Good Answers

"If you, then, though you are evil, know how to give good
gifts to your children, how much more will your Father
in heaven give good gifts to those who ask him!"

MATTHEW 7:11 NIV

You've prayed and prayed, and now God has finally gifted
you with an answer. But perhaps it wasn't the answer you
were seeking. Or perhaps it seems like God has been silent, the
answer coming long after you thought it should. It's easy to let
your thoughts slip into questioning God and His wisdom. After
all, don't you know exactly what you need?

That's when it's time to remind yourself of Matthew 7:11:
If earthly parents know how to give good gifts to their children, don't you think God—the perfect Father—knows how
to give the very best gifts to you? So perhaps this gift He's
given you doesn't seem so good right now. But wait, and trust,
and you will see: God's answer will be the gift you needed, even
if it isn't the gift you wanted.

*Lord, I know that You always answer my
prayers. Open my eyes and my heart to the
perfect goodness of Your answers, even when
I don't yet understand them. Amen.*

Where Is God?

The LORD is good, a refuge in times of trouble.
He cares for those who trust in him.

NAHUM 1:7 NIV

Everyone goes through times of trouble, whether it's for days, months, or even years. Dealing with them is just part of living in this fallen world. So where is the grace in that? Where is God's goodness when everything around you seems so bad? Where is God?

He has never left your side; He is right there with you. As Deuteronomy 31:8 (NIV) tells us, "The LORD himself goes before you and will be with you; he will never leave you nor forsake you. Do not be afraid; do not be discouraged."

God's grace will give you His strength and comfort; "The LORD will fight for you; you need only to be still" (Exodus 14:14 NIV). And you will find His goodness in the inexplicable peace—a peace "which transcends all understanding"—that floods your soul as you seek refuge in His welcoming arms (Philippians 4:7 NIV).

Lord God, when troubles seem to come at me from every side, remind me to run to You—my Refuge, the One Who cares for me. Amen.

Lost in the Wonder

*I will meditate on your majestic, glorious splendor
and your wonderful miracles.*
PSALM 145:5 NLT

I t's so easy to get bogged down in the millions of little details that make up your daily life. Pay the bills. Wash the clothes. Meet the deadline. Cook the dinner. Go. Pick up. Clean up. Get up.

Sometimes you just need to stop, and . . . *breathe*.

Take a day, an hour, or even just a moment to look around at the glorious splendor of God's creation. Let yourself get lost in the wonder of it all. See that sunlight? God *spoke*, and it soared across the universe to brighten the sky. See that tree? God planted that tree within a seed and then told it how and when to grow. And that face staring back at you in the mirror? God breathed life into your soul and declared you "amazing and wonderful" (Psalm 139:14 NCV).

In the midst of the million little things that clutter up each day, don't forget to stop once in a while to breathe . . . and to get lost in the wonder.

*Lord, it's so easy to forget the wonder of Your
might and majesty in the midst of the daily slog.
Open my eyes to Your wonder all around me,
especially in the ordinary things. Amen.*

A Song in the Night

The LORD will send his faithful love by day;
his song will be with me in the night—
a prayer to the God of my life.

PSALM 42:8 CSB

G od is faithful, sending His love to you every day. In the bright sunlight of the day, it's easier to remember that you are not alone, that His love and presence are with you in whatever troubles come your way.

But in the darkness of night, when the shadows of worry and fear and doubt creep about you, stalking you like prey, it's harder to see His light. This is when God sends you His song—to fill your mind with a sweet reminder that He is near. Whether it's a joyful lullaby to softly carry you to sleep or a song of trust to still the storms so you can rest, listen . . . and let the words of His song become your prayer to the God who cradles your life in His hands.

Lord, Your grace is in the song You give me in the shadows of the night. Teach me to hear the words and to lift them up to You in trusting praise. Amen.

Grace Is Busy

Be doers of the word, and not hearers only . . .

JAMES 1:22 NKJV

G race is busy. It always has been.

It was Jesus's grace that saved the adulterous woman when the Pharisees wanted to stone her—saving her life and her soul (John 8). It was His grace that lifted Peter up out of the waves (Matthew 14). It was His grace that had compassion and then moved to teach and touch, to love and heal.

Because grace doesn't sit idly by while others suffer or struggle. It doesn't stand around waiting for something to happen, to be pulled into action, or for someone else to do what needs to be done. Grace sees the need and steps in. That's what Jesus did. It's what His grace does for you, and it's what you can do for Him.

Be His hands. Be His feet. Don't sit idly by while others struggle. See the need, step in, and let God's grace be busy through you.

Lord, show me how I can step in and help someone today. Let me never forget to give back the grace that I've been given. Amen.

Grace Is Rest

*"Come to me, all you who are weary and
burdened, and I will give you rest."*

<small>MATTHEW 11:28 NIV</small>

Yes, grace is busy. But, in one of those beautiful impossibilities of God, grace is also rest.

When grace is busy, weariness can seep in. Ingratitude from those you serve, to-do lists that are just too long, the exhaustion of giving to others all day long—all these take their toll.

Take time to rest a little each day in the arms of your Savior. Let yourself accept the grace that He lavishes upon you.

Go to Him. Lay your worries, your doubts and fears, and those far-too-heavy burdens at His feet. Let Him to carry the load. Close your eyes and rest your head upon His heart. Remember who He is and who you are in Him. Remember why you do all that you do. Let Him heal your heart and steel you with His strength . . . so that grace can be busy again.

*Lord, there is so much I need to do today,
so much I want to do, but help me never
to get too busy to rest in You. Amen.*

JANUARY 13

Ask God

Send out your light and your truth;
let them guide me.
Let them lead me to your holy mountain,
to the place where you live.
PSALM 43:3 NLT

We have so many different decisions to make. Some are small—what to eat, what to wear, how to spend your evening. Others can change the course of your life, or even your eternity. Which choice should you make? Which path should you take?

Ask God.

When you're not sure what your decision should be—or even when you believe that you are—ask God to guide you. Ask God to light up the way you should go with the truth of His Word. God's wisdom is yours for the asking, for He "gives generously to all without finding fault, and it will be given to you" (James 1:5 NIV). He won't show you every detail of the journey, but He'll show you the next step to take . . . and then the next . . . and the next.

Trust Him to guide you. Hold fast to His hand. And He'll lead you all the way home with Him.

 Lord, I thank You for the gift of Your wisdom. Please shine Your light into my life today and guide me in the way You would have me go. Amen.

El Roi

She gave this name to the Lord who spoke to
her: "You are the God who sees me," for she said,
"I have now seen the One who sees me."
GENESIS 16:13 NIV

*E*l Roi. God sees you.

God saw Hagar, the runaway servant girl of Abraham and Sarah, alone and frightened in the desert, and He helped her. He saw the widow at the Temple drop in her two tiny coins—all she had to give—and He praised her. He saw Mary weeping by the empty tomb, and He came to comfort her.

And God sees *you*. When you're frightened and alone, when you're giving everything you have to give and no one seems to care, when you're feeling swallowed up by the sorrows of this world, God sees you. When no one else notices your tears, knows your hopes, or understands your dreams, God notices and knows and understands. You are never invisible to Him—not now, not ever. He is *El Roi*. And He sees you, today and always.

*Lord, sometimes I feel invisible, as if no one
knows or cares or understands. But You do.
Thank You for always seeing me, for always
noticing, and knowing, and loving. Amen.*

The Throne of Grace

Let us therefore come boldly to the throne of grace, that we may obtain mercy and find grace to help in time of need.

HEBREWS 4:16 NKJV

When we decide to follow Jesus, we are given an amazing gift: an audience with the King of kings. And this isn't just a onetime gift; it's an anytime, all-the-time gift. That means you can step right into the very throne room of God and speak to the Lord of All Creation, morning or noon, day or night, for as long as you like and as often as you like.

There's no waiting in line. There's no tiptoeing about. There's no question of whether or not you will be seen. You can be bold when you come before God's throne of grace. And what do you find there? Not some cold and distant ruler, but rather your loving Father who offers mercy for your sins and mistakes and helps in your time of need. Bow your head in prayer; step before His throne.

 God, You are the Lord of lords and King of kings. There is none more powerful than You. And yet You are always ready to listen, to lead, and to help me. Thank You for hearing my prayers. Amen.

God Calls You by Name

"Do not be afraid . . .
I have called you by name; you are mine."

ISAIAH 43:1 NLT

God is infinite. He is "the Alpha and the Omega," both beginning and end (Revelation 1:8 NIV). His power is unimaginable—He set the sun and moon in their places in the heavens (Genesis 1:16–17). And His knowledge is all-encompassing: "He determines the number of the stars and calls them each by name" (Psalm 147:4 NIV).

And this same God knows *your* name. In this world, you will face many troubling things, but you don't ever have to be afraid. Because the Lord and Creator of this vast universe is also the Lord and Creator of you. He knows you, and He calls you by your name. And then He declares for all of creation, all of eternity to hear: *"You are Mine!"* We have nothing to be afraid of.

Lord, when I look up at the night sky and see all those stars, it's hard to believe that the One Who created those also knows me. But I do believe. You call me by name, and I praise You. Amen.

Pure Light

This is the message we heard from Jesus and now declare to
you: God is light, and there is no darkness in him at all.

1 JOHN 1:5 NLT

There is a darkness in this world that has nothing to do with a lack of sunlight, firelight, or lamplight. Sometimes it's so thick it seems as though you can almost reach out your hand and touch the inky blackness. Other times, the light seems brilliant and bright, but it is still touched by shadows. In this fallen world, and even in each of us, there is always a touch of darkness.

But there is no darkness in God. Not one shadow, not one smudge of gray. He is pure truth, pure love, and pure light. And the closer you draw to Him, the more the darkness shrinks away. "Draw near to God and He will draw near to you," says James 4:8 (NKJV). "Cleanse *your* hands, *you* sinners; and purify *your* hearts, *you* double-minded."

Step into the light of God's grace and linger there today.

Holy Father, please forgive me for the darkness
inside of me, and help me to face the darkness
in the world with You beside me. Cleanse me,
Lord, with the pure light of Your grace. Amen.

God at Work

> God was kind! He made me what I am, and his
> wonderful kindness wasn't wasted. I worked much
> harder than any of the other apostles, although it
> was really God's kindness at work and not me.
>
> 1 CORINTHIANS 15:10 CEV

Although Paul wrote the words of this verse thousands of years ago, they could just as easily be written by us today. The apostle Paul worked hard to be the best follower of Christ that he could be. Perhaps that was because he knew how much he had been forgiven. But Paul also knew that no matter how hard he worked, any goodness within him was not of his own doing. It was because God was working in him.

As children of God, everything we are—everything we do and have, every drop of goodness within us—is a result of God working in us. Because He created us in His own image and gifted us with our every talent, every ability, and every opportunity. Yes, we work hard, but it is the kindness of God at work within us that makes us who we are.

*Lord God, I know that everything good within
me, every good thing I am able to do, is because
of You working in my life. Work in me this day,
Lord, and make me more like You. Amen.*

Waiting on God

I waited patiently for the LORD;
he turned to me and heard my cry.
He lifted me out of the slimy pit,
out of the mud and mire;
he set my feet on a rock
and gave me a firm place to stand.

PSALM 40:1–2 NIV

No one likes to wait, especially if you happen to be waiting on a rescue. Sometimes, though, that's exactly what God asks you to do. And not just wait, but wait *patiently*, which implies that you just might be waiting for a while.

But waiting on God isn't like waiting in a checkout line that may close, waiting on a call that may never come, or waiting on a flight that may be delayed or even canceled. Waiting on God comes with a promise: He *will* answer. He *will* rescue you out of that slimy pit, wash away the mud and mire, and give you a firm place to stand. So don't be frightened by the wait. God's rescue will come in His own perfect time, in His own perfect way.

*Lord, waiting is so hard. Please help my heart to trust
You and Your ways as I wait for Your rescue. Amen.*

A New Song to Sing

He put a new song in my mouth,
a hymn of praise to our God.
Many will see and fear the LORD
and put their trust in him.

PSALM 40:3 NIV

G od hears our cries for help. That truth alone is wonderful, because to simply be heard in this world of noise is a powerful thing. But God doesn't *just* listen. He rescues. He reaches down from the heights of heaven to lift us out of the depths of our troubles and sorrows (Psalm 40:2).

And that would be enough, wouldn't it? To be heard *and* to be rescued. But God doesn't stop there. He also gives us a reason to sing. He fills our minds, our hearts, our souls, and our lives with the beauty of His truth, shaping it into words that spill out in the praises of song. And as we sing, others will learn to see and trust the God Who hears and rescues and brings us joy.

Lord, fill my mind and my mouth with songs of praise this day for all the wonders You have done in my life. Amen.

The Lord Listens

I love the LORD because he hears my voice
and my prayer for mercy.
Because he bends down to listen,
I will pray as long as I have breath!

PSALM 116:1–2 NLT

Have you ever considered all the sounds that God must have to listen to? The sounds of His creation, the songs of the angels, the prayers of all His people. How could He possibly hear you . . . *just you?*

Yet that's exactly what He does. When you pray to the Lord in heaven, He hears *your* voice. He hears every word you say—shouted, whispered, or silently pleaded from your heart. And more than that, He "bends down to listen." Imagine . . . it's as if the God of all creation hears that first word of your prayer and says, "Shhh! My child is speaking." Then He cups a hand around His ear and bends down low . . . because He doesn't want to miss one single, precious word.

What will you say to Him today?

As long as I have breath, I will pray to You, Lord.
Because You bend down to listen, even to me. Amen.

Delight in the Details

The LORD directs the steps of the godly.
He delights in every detail of their lives.

PSALM 37:23 NLT

D o you know anyone who delights in *every* aspect of your life, even the most hidden parts? In even the closest relationships, people are seldom interested in knowing every detail. But God is. Your joy over that small success, those hurt feelings you're trying so hard to hide, that dream you haven't dared to share with a single soul—God knows them all and delights in them all.

Because God knows all the details—all your hopes and dreams, all your fears and worries, all your joys and heartaches— because He knows the deepest and truest needs of your heart, God knows the path you should follow to bring you home to Him. And He lovingly directs your steps, delighting in your presence all along the way.

Please guide me, Lord, through every step of this life so that I may always be a delight to You. Amen.

Help the Ones You Love

*A funeral procession was coming out as [Jesus]
approached the village gate. The young man
who had died was a widow's only son . . .*

LUKE 7:12 NLT

As Jesus approached the gate of the village of Nain, He was met by a funeral procession. A woman—a widow—had lost her only son. While the loss of her son was, in itself, a heartbreaking tragedy, his death practically guaranteed her poverty and a future of desperation. When Jesus saw her sorrow, His own heart was filled with compassion for this hurting one whom He loved. "Don't cry," He comforted her.

And then He stepped over to the coffin, touched it to stop the procession, and commanded the young man to get up . . . and he did! Jesus gave the mother back her son.

Jesus taught many lessons—important and eternal lessons—in the synagogues, in the homes of His followers, on the plain, and on the mount. But one of His greatest lessons was this: Help the ones you love.

*Lord, open my heart to the sorrow around
me and show me something I can do today
to help those whom I love. Amen.*

The Goodness of God

The LORD passed in front of Moses, calling out,
"Yahweh! The LORD!
The God of compassion and mercy!
I am slow to anger
and filled with unfailing love and faithfulness."
EXODUS 34:6 NLT

Grace is the goodness of God at work in our lives. And, let's be honest, it's a work He didn't have to do. After all, He gave us our very lives. He gave us this world to live in. He gave us laws to follow. And when we broke them—when we continue to break them—God could have washed His hands of us. But He didn't. He doesn't. And, best of all, He *won't*.

God chooses to continually pour out His goodness upon us, His children, *and* upon those He wants to call His children. He is "merciful and gracious" and inexplicably patient with us. His goodness knows no boundaries—nothing "will be able to separate us from the love of God that is in Christ Jesus our Lord" (Romans 8:39 NIV). That's grace. That's Who God is. And that's what He does in our lives.

*Lord, I place so many limits on my own mercy
and patience with others that it's hard to believe
You can be so patient with me. Open my eyes to
see Your grace at work in my life today. Amen.*

Thunder from Heaven

The Lord thundered from heaven;
the voice of the Most High resounded
amid the hail and burning coals.
He shot his arrows and scattered his enemies . . .

PSALM 18:13–14 NLT

Who holds your faith? Stop for a moment and really think about that question. Is your faith in the power of the enemy to wreck and ruin? Or is your faith in the power of God to overcome and utterly defeat the enemy?

Because, yes, the devil is powerful. He's on the prowl "like a roaring lion looking for someone to devour" (1 Peter 5:8 NIV). But when you choose to put your faith in God, to trust and obey and follow Him, then the full power and might and majesty of God Himself comes thundering down from heaven to defend you. Yes, you will have troubles in this world. Yes, the enemy will tempt and trick and try to trap. But always remember this: "He who is in you is greater than he who is in the world" (1 John 4:4 NKJV), and His victory is already won, through Christ.

*Holy Father, when the enemy attacks and when
my faith wavers, remind me of who You are and
the victory You have already won for me. Amen.*

Just as You Are

A woman in that town who lived a sinful life learned
that Jesus was eating at the Pharisee's house, so she
came there with an alabaster jar of perfume. As she
stood behind him at his feet weeping, she began to wet
his feet with her tears. Then she wiped them with her
hair, kissed them and poured perfume on them. . . .
Jesus said to the woman, "Your faith has saved you; go in peace."

LUKE 7:37–38, 50 NIV

She knew who she was, and she knew—far better than
anyone—the things she had done. And when she stepped
inside that Pharisee's house, she knew that they knew too. But
this woman had come to see her Savior, and not even their
scorn could keep her away. Falling at His feet, her tears told
Jesus all He needed to know about her heart.

She had come to give Jesus a gift, but He gave her a far greater
one. Because grace doesn't demand that you be perfect before falling at the feet of the Savior. Grace welcomes you just as you are
and then begins perfecting your heart. It tells us that "he who
began a good work in you will carry it on to completion . . ." (Philippians 1:6 NIV). All you have to do is come . . . and fall at His feet.

*Holy Lord Jesus, I come now and fall at
Your feet. Please wash away my sins and
cover me with Your grace. Amen.*

God Knows . . . and Remembers

You keep track of all my sorrows.
You have collected all my tears in your bottle.
You have recorded each one in your book.
PSALM 56:8 NLT

When people ask, you smile and say, "I'm fine." You don't drop the mask or let them see what's really going on. You don't tell them about the hurts, the worries, the fears. You don't let them see your tears. And because you don't tell and because you don't let anyone see, you start to think no one knows. But God knows.

Every wandering of fear and doubt and worry. God tracks them all. He keeps a record, he stores them away . . . and God *remembers* when you have been frightened or hurt. And what does God do? He hurts with you (Isaiah 63:9). He weeps with you (John 11:35). And then He comes to comfort, strengthen, and rescue you (Psalm 145:19).

So the next time you find yourself saying "I'm fine" when you're anything but, remember that God sees and knows—and He's coming to comfort you.

Lord God, thank You for seeing my tears, for knowing
my sorrows. Help me remember that I never have
to try to hide my true feelings, fears, and hurts from
You—the One Who can truly heal me. Amen.

Taming the Lion

"Stay alert! Watch out for your great enemy,
the devil. He prowls around like a roaring
lion, looking for someone to devour."

1 PETER 5:8 NLT

Y ou have an enemy—and it's not that grouchy neighbor across the street or that gossip in the corner cubicle. This enemy is far more powerful. He likes to trip you up by piling up frustrations that tempt you to lose your temper. He likes to toss obstacles in your path to make you stumble and say that word, do that thing you know you shouldn't do. And he likes to lie— one of his favorite tricks—to make you think you're somehow beyond the reach of God's love and grace.

Stay alert! Watch out and be ever on your guard. But don't be afraid or worried. Because here's the good news (and Daniel can vouch for Him): God's great at taming lions. In fact, He's just waiting to toss this one back into his cage.

*Lord, I know the devil is just waiting for a
chance to trip me up today. Help me to keep
my eyes open to his lies and tricks. . . . I trust
You to put that lion back in his cage.*

What If . . . ?

"My Presence will go with you, and I will give you rest."
EXODUS 33:14 NIV

It's been a long, hard day . . . or week, or month, or season of life. And you are so very tired. Shoulders aching with the burden, struggling to keep putting one foot in front of the other. But there's so much more to do, so you force yourself to push through the weariness. No time for God, no time for prayer, and certainly no time for you. You have to get it together, keep it together, and keep going. But what if you didn't?

What if you said no? That thing can wait, but God can't. What if you stepped out of the rat race and stepped into the presence of God, handed over all those burdens, closed your eyes, and let Him give you rest. Because that's just what Christ promises to do when we come to Him (Matthew 11:28). And then, when you're ready to step back into the world, He will be right by your side, every step of the way.

Lord, when I am exhausted and overwhelmed,
remind me that it's okay to step away
and seek rest in You. Amen.

The Good News

"When you go through deep waters,
I will be with you.
When you go through rivers of difficulty,
you will not drown.
When you walk through the fire of oppression,
you will not be burned up;
the flames will not consume you."

ISAIAH 43:2 NLT

In a world that is so full of bad news, aren't you ready for something good? You'll find it in the most unlikely of places: right in the middle of the bad.

Jesus promised us that "in this world you will have trouble" (John 16:33 NIV). And although this promise doesn't usually make our list of favorites, there will be deep waters of sorrow, rivers of difficulty, and fires of oppression—along with the million and one other frustrations and exasperations of living life in a world filled with sin.

But here's the good news, *the best news*: God is here, even within this pain. His strength keeps us afloat and doesn't allow us to drown in the difficulties. Yes, there is always trouble. "But take heart!" Jesus says. "I have overcome the world" (John 16:33 NIV).

Lord, when I struggle today with the bad news, remind
me of the good news: that You are with me—and Your
goodness is mightier than the badness. Amen.

31

Never Forgotten

"See, I have written your name on the palms of my hands."
ISAIAH 49:16 NLT

Your coworker forgot to mention your contribution to the project. Your best friend forgot your birthday. Even your mom forgot your lunch date. It happens—days when we feel completely overlooked.

But there is One Who finds it impossible to forget you: God. "Can a mother forget her nursing child?" He asks. "Can she feel no love for the child she has borne? But even if that were possible, I would not forget you!" (Isaiah 49:15 NLT). You see, the One who knows the name of each and every star (Psalm 147:4) knows your name. And more than that, He has written it on the palms of His hands, in eternal ink.

So close your eyes for a moment and savor this truth: When God looks down at His hands—those same hands that scattered the stars—He sees *your* name, and He remembers how much He loves *you*.

Lord, I am in awe of what You have done and what You have created. But when I remember You have written my name on Your hands, I am even more amazed. Thank You for remembering me always. Amen.

FEBRUARY

You've Got a Friend

"I no longer call you servants, because servants don't know what their master is doing. But now I call you friends, because I have told you everything that my Father told me."

JOHN 15:15 ERV

Whether you're alone in a new city or alone in a crowd, whether you've lost someone you love or have just never figured out how to fit in, life can be lonely when you don't have a friend.

That's when it's time to remember this beautiful truth: You are never truly without a friend. And not just *a* friend but *the* Friend. Jesus knows everything about you and still wants to be with you. And because He knows everything about you, He is able to comfort you, guide you, and love you *perfectly*.

Jesus chooses you to be His friend. But just like the notes we once passed in elementary school, you also get to choose to be His. Will you check *Yes* or *No*?

Lord Jesus, I praise You for the overwhelming gift of Your friendship. And, yes, I choose You—today and every day—to be my Friend. Amen.

When You're a Friend of Jesus

"You are my friends, if you obey me."

JOHN 15:14 CEV

Jesus has chosen you to be His friend, and you have chosen Him in return. But what does a friendship with Jesus look like when you rise up in the morning, when you step out into the day, and when you lay your head down to sleep at night?

The answer is *obedience*. It's not the most popular word in the dictionary these days, but it's the foundation of your friendship with Christ. When you're a friend of Jesus's, you don't obey Him mindlessly or thoughtlessly. Rather, you obey Him because He tells you *why* you should: because He wants you to live forever with Him. So be fair to others, be just, kind, and humble (Micah 6:8), and love Him "with all your heart and with all your soul and with all your mind and with all your strength" (Mark 12:30 NIV). That's what friends of Jesus do.

Lord, teach me as I walk through this day what it means to be Your friend. And lead me to others that I can introduce to You. Amen.

Enough Light to See

"No one lights a lamp and then covers it with a bowl or hides it under a bed. Instead, they put the lamp on a lampstand so that the people who come in will have enough light to see."

LUKE 8:16 ERV

How much light is enough light to see? A verse read, a prayer shared, a meal delivered—all of these things shine a spark of God's light. The spark from a single match can pour light into a darkened room.

But why limit yourself? Why be a spark when you can be a flame? And why be a flame when you can be a raging fire? Consider the gifts, the talents, and the blessings God has given you. They're yours for a reason—to use for His kingdom.

How can you use what you've been given to shine the light of God into the darkness of this world today? Do some thinking, get creative, make a list. And then shine your light bright enough for others to see the way to God and His amazing grace.

Lord, please show me how I can use the gifts You've given me to shine a light so bright others can't help but see You. Amen.

The Freedom of Grace

*Sin is no longer your master, for you no longer
live under the requirements of the law. Instead,
you live under the freedom of God's grace.*

ROMANS 6:14 NLT

In the Torah—the first five books of the Old Testament—God gives the people of Israel more than six hundred different laws. There are some who claim that sin was the result of too many different laws to keep track of.

But the real reason for the sin in our lives isn't the number of laws we're given to obey. After all, Jesus wrapped them all up in just two commandments: "'Love the Lord your God with all your heart and with all your soul and with all your mind'" is the first, "and the second is like it: 'Love your neighbor as yourself'" (Matthew 22:37, 39 NIV).

We sin because we would rather do what *we* want than what *God* wants. Amazingly, God knows our stubborn hearts, and yet He still wants us with Him. And that's why He sent Jesus: to offer us stubborn slaves to sin the freedom of His grace.

*Dear Lord, forgive my stubbornness and my
selfishness. In everything I do and say today, help
me to strive to please You and not just me. Amen.*

A Way Out

You are tempted in the same way that everyone else is tempted.
But God can be trusted not to let you be tempted too much,
and he will show you how to escape from your temptations.

1 CORINTHIANS 10:13 CEV

Each of us must deal with temptation, often on a daily, hourly, even minute-by-minute basis. And the temptations are unique to each of us, specially designed by the enemy to target our weaknesses.

If you struggle with pride, the enemy will attack your ego. If you struggle with greed, money is his weapon of choice. And if gossip is your weakness, the devil is sure to find some juicy tidbit to dangle in front of you. But even though the evil one is able to tailor the temptations to you, he can't force you to give in to them. There is a way to escape temptation's trap: Turn to God, trust Him, and He'll show you a way out.

Lord, when temptation comes my way
today, remind me to turn to You. I know
You'll help me find a way out. Amen.

Hands and Feet

"Look at my hands. Look at my feet.
You can see that it's really me."

LUKE 24:39 NLT

When Jesus rose up from the grave, He went to His disciples and showed them the wounds in His hands so that they would believe—so that they would know it was really Him.

In today's world, we can't see His hands or His feet the way the disciples did. But we can see what those hands and feet did. His hands touched the leper and the lame. They lifted up praise to God, and they reached down to lift a fallen woman to her feet. His feet carried Him to sinners' homes, to a mount and a plain, and a well in Samaria. They carried Him to Jerusalem, knowing that the cross lay before Him.

No, we can't see Jesus's hands and feet, but we can see that they did. And today we can try to do a little bit of the same.

Lord, teach me to be Jesus's hands and feet. To touch the sick and hurting, to lift up the fallen, to go into the world to tell others about You. Amen.

Delighted

He led me to a place of safety;
he rescued me because he delights in me.

PSALM 18:19 NLT

I f words could smile, "delight" would be a big, toothy grin.

What delights you? Ice cream cones dripping lazily in the summer's heat? The laughter of children floating across the playground? Pressing SEND on that project you've been pouring yourself into for weeks?

Think about the things that delight you, and then ask yourself, *What delights God?* He tells us. God is delighted when we do what is right (Micah 6:8), when we take care of widows and orphans (James 1:27), love our neighbor (Matthew 22:39), and, of course, love Him (Matthew 22:37).

But there's one more thing that delights God, and you don't want to miss it. Because that one thing is . . . *you.* Not because you're perfect; not because of anything you've said or done. Simply because you're you. So whatever happens to you, remember this: God sent His own Son to rescue you and to lead you to safety because He is delighted by you.

Holy Father, how wonderful it is to know
that You find delight in me. Please help me to
live a life that makes You smile. Amen.

Searching for You

"Suppose one of you has a hundred sheep but loses one of them. Then he will leave the other ninety-nine sheep in the open field and go out and look for the lost sheep until he finds it."

LUKE 15:4 NCV

When you wander away, the God who spoke all the world into being searches for you.

Perhaps it's not that you've turned your back on God or that you're upset with Him. Perhaps it's simply busyness that's taken you away. Distracted by the never-ending demands of to-do lists, projects, and overwhelming obligations, you think there just isn't time for God too. Not today. Maybe tomorrow. But then tomorrow comes and pulls at you with its own set of impossible-to-finish tasks.

Whether you've wandered away for one moment or for many, God sends out the alarm. But He doesn't send His angels to look for you. No. God searches for you *Himself.* And when He finds you—when you allow yourself to be found—He picks you up and joyfully brings you home.

O Father, forgive me for the times I allow busyness to pull me away from You. Show me today what is truly important and what I can let go of—so that I can hold tight to You. Amen.

His Glory

"Please, show me Your glory."

EXODUS 33:18 NKJV

S ometimes we just need to see—with our own eyes, our own hearts—the glory of God in our lives. Moses did. Because God was asking Moses to do some pretty big things, and because the Israelites were being . . . well, altogether too stubbornly human. Moses wasn't so much testing God as he was asking for a little reassurance—a little light.

No matter how big or small the task God has set before you, we can all use a bit of reassurance sometimes. And the beautiful thing is that when you ask God to show Himself, He will. In His own perfect way, God will reveal that He is indeed at work in your life. It might not be the way you expect, so pay attention. Look and listen with your heart, for God often moves quietly and speaks in whispers. Still, God will show you His glory, and it usually looks a lot like grace.

Lord, I know You are working in my life, and I trust You to work in the ways that are best for me. But I could use a little reassurance. Help me see Your presence today. Amen.

Questions

Then the woman of Samaria said to Him, "How is it that You, being a Jew, ask a drink from me, a Samaritan woman?"

JOHN 4:9 NKJV

I magine the scene: Jesus, the Son of God, road weary and thirsty, sitting by a well. The Samaritan woman, who should have been invisible to a Jewish man, coming to draw water. There should have been zero conversation. But there was. And not just any conversation: The Samaritan woman was bold. She had questions. "How?" "Where?" "Why?"

Jesus didn't scold her for her questions. Instead, he gave her answers.

And He won't scold you for your questions, either. Not the how, the where, or the why. If you have a question, go to Jesus—in prayer and in His Word. He will give you living water, just as He did for the woman by the well.

Be alert to the possibility of a conversation today, especially a highly unexpected one. A conversation like this may lead to questions that then lead to answers . . . that then lead a thirsty soul to the living water of God.

Thank You, Lord, for welcoming my questions.
Help me to listen and to hear Your answers. Amen.

The God of Hope

*May the God of hope fill you with all joy and
peace as you trust in him, so that you may overflow
with hope by the power of the Holy Spirit.*

ROMANS 15:13 NIV

The Lord is the God of hope, not of defeat or despair. And
His hope is not of wished-for dreams that may or may not
come true. Instead, the hope of our God is one of promises that
will be fulfilled: "He is the faithful God, keeping his covenant
of love to a thousand generations of those who love him and
keep his commandments" (Deuteronomy 7:9 NIV).

When you look around you today and wonder what it is
that God really wants for you—in the midst of the chaos of
carpools, conference calls, and grocery store trips—know that
He wants you to have hope. Hope of joy. Hope of peace. Hope
of His power working in your life.

And hope is exactly what God promises to give you. Not
because you've earned it, but because of His grace.

*Lord, You are a God of hope. Teach me what
that really means in my life—and show me how
to help others find Your hope too. Amen.*

Refuge

God is our refuge and strength,
an ever-present help in trouble.

PSALM 46:1 NIV

A refuge is a place to run to, a place to hide away in, where you can be safe. It's somewhere impenetrable and mighty (Psalm 46:1 AMP). This is exactly what you will find in the presence of God, but it isn't all. For His refuge is also a place to be renewed—not with your own oh-so-limited strength, but with His unending power.

This refuge and strength are yours to claim—always. Not just when you think you have your act together, and not just when you're at the end of your rope with nowhere else to turn. It doesn't matter if today's trouble is massive or minuscule. The help of God is ever-present, and it is always available to you.

*Lord, I am so grateful for the peace, the strength,
and the help I find when I take refuge in You.
Forgive me for the times I don't run to You. Amen.*

When You Think of God . . .

*Now Christ Jesus has come to show us the kindness of God.
Christ our Savior defeated death and brought us the good
news. It shines like a light and offers life that never ends.*

2 TIMOTHY 1:10 CEV

When you think of God, what words come to your mind first? Perhaps you think of "holy," "powerful," "mighty," or "majestic." But what about "kind"?

Because, yes, God is awesome, holy, mighty, and majestic—but He is also unfailingly kind. It was kindness that spoke to the woman by the well. It was kindness that touched the lepers and made them whole. And it was kindness that lifted a no-longer-bleeding woman to her feet and called her "daughter" (Matthew 9:20–22 NIV).

That same kindness is still there for us today, shining like a light and offering life that never ends. It is ours to take. We call it grace.

*Lord, when I struggle to be kind, help me
remember the power of Your kindness and all that
it has done—and still does—for me. Amen.*

Real Love

This is what real love is: It is not our love for
God; it is God's love for us. He sent his Son to
die in our place to take away our sins.

1 JOHN 4:10 NCV

Real love isn't flowers or candy. It's isn't pretty words or passionate kisses. It looks nothing like greeting cards or commercials or Hollywood movies.

Real love isn't pretty. It looks like arms stretched wide on a cross, wearing a crown of thorns and a cloak of suffering. Think about what that took, not just for Jesus who suffered and died, but for God. He sent His Son, whom He dearly loved, to this earth. He knew what Jesus would endure. God sent Him not only for the people who loved Him but also for the people who didn't love Him—and never would. He sent His son to give us grace.

This is the real love that the Father has for you—a love that welcomes you into His family.

Father, I look at the cross and I see how much You
love me. Let my life be a living "Thank You" for
the gift, the grace You've given me. Amen.

A Love That Gives

My Lord, your love is real.

PSALM 62:12 ERV

Merriam-Webster.com defines "love" as a "strong affection" based on "kinship or personal ties," "admiration," or "common interests." In Hebrew, the word used above in Psalm 62 is חֶסֶד (*chesed*). It means favor, goodness, and kindness; it's sometimes translated as "mercy" or "loving-kindness."

Do you see the difference? The world sees love as something that centers around you rather than the one you love. It's focused on what your connection is: what you admire and what you desire. It's more about taking. But *chesed* centers on what God gives to you: His favor, His goodness, His mercy and loving-kindness.

God's love for you is grace.

Lord, thank You for the real love You pour into my life. Help me to offer that same kind of selfless love back to You and to those around me. Amen.

Happily Ever After

And so we will be with the Lord forever.

1 THESSALONIANS 4:17 NIV

Who doesn't love a fairy tale with a good "happily ever after"? The damsel in distress is rescued by Prince Charming, who then defeats the villain and saves the land. Or, in the more modern takes, the damsel rescues herself and lends Prince Charming a hand. But we all know that in the real world, there are no perfect "happily ever afters." Right?

Wrong.

Once upon a time, God sent His Son to rescue a people in distress. He conquered the villains of sin and death and the devil. And as He stretched His arms open wide, He offered His people a promise: Follow Me and live happily ever after. That's no fairy tale. That's grace.

Lord, You offer me the one true "happily ever after." And I accept it . . . today, tomorrow, and always. Thank You, Lord. Amen.

Even Your Enemies

"But I tell you, love your enemies . . ."
MATTHEW 5:44 NIV

*L*ove my enemies? But, Jesus, you don't understand what she did or what he said . . .

Oh, but Jesus does understand. Never forget that this is the Jesus who stooped to wash the feet of His betrayer. This is the Jesus who cried out from the cross, interceding with the Father for the very ones who put Him there: "Father, forgive them, for they do not know what they do" (Luke 23:34 NKJV). This is the Jesus who left heaven to transform you from a sin-stained enemy of God to an adopted heir of heaven.

Love even your enemies. It's a grace God asks us to give others because it's a grace He's given to us.

Lord, sin made me Your enemy, yet You still chose to love me. Help me to do the same—to love my enemies—because You love me. Amen.

Hemmed In

You hem me in behind and before,
and you lay your hand upon me.

PSALM 139:5 NIV

Being hemmed in sounds like something that the bad guys in a movie might do: constrictive, isolating, and dangerous. But when God is doing the hemming, it's anything but bad. Instead, it provides us the ultimate security.

Whatever kind of day you're having—good or bad or somewhere in between—you are utterly hemmed in and surrounded by the goodness of God.

He goes before you into the future so that you'll be prepared for what lies ahead. He walks behind you, covering the sins and mistakes of the past with His grace. And He stands with you today in this moment, holding tight to you with His own hand.

Pause now for a moment. Look around and see the goodness of God that hems you in so completely.

Lord, thank You for hemming me in with
Your presence. Teach my eyes to see Your
goodness all around me. Amen.

Worth It

Christ loved us and gave himself up for us . . .
EPHESIANS 5:2 NIV

Everywhere you turn, there's sure to be someone telling you that you don't have what it takes. Maybe your parents made it clear you weren't the favorite child; or childhood classmates who never picked you for their team; or the boss who keeps passing you over for the promotion; or the endless advertisements that whisper that you're too fat, too thin, too old, too young, too much, or too little.

There's no shortage of those willing to tell you that, for whatever reason they care to make up, you're just not worthy. But hear this today: God, the Great "I AM," the Alpha and the Omega, the One Who lit up the universe with a word, says, "You're worth it." You were worth leaving heaven for, worth dying for, and worth loving for all eternity. Believe Him, not them.

Lord, forgive me for letting the world tell me my worth. Remind me that I am worth everything to You, the One who created the world. Amen.

Perfected

Let us run with perseverance the race marked out for us,
fixing our eyes on Jesus, the pioneer and perfecter of faith.
For the joy set before him he endured the cross, scorning its
shame, and sat down at the right hand of the throne of God.

HEBREWS 12:1–2 NIV

No matter how hard you try, you won't ever be perfect. It doesn't matter how many straight As you get, or how many strikes in your bowling scores, or how spotless your house is. When it comes to the things that really matter—the things that *eternally* matter—you won't ever be able to make yourself perfect.

But one day you will be *made* perfect—not by your own efforts but by Jesus's.

You see, Jesus looked at the cross and then He looked at you. He endured that cross so that you could be perfected and so that He could experience the joy of spending forever with you. So take a deep breath. You don't have to be perfect, because you have been perfected by Jesus.

Lord, I know that no matter how hard I try,
I will never be perfect enough for heaven.
That's why I'm so thankful for Your grace that
covers over all my imperfections. Amen.

Thoughtfully and Intentionally

*Every good and perfect gift is from above, coming
down from the Father of the heavenly lights,
who does not change like shifting shadows.*

JAMES 1:17 NIV

Whatever your income level or your socioeconomic status may be, you are richly blessed. It's easy to lose sight of that truth and to stop noticing all the blessings you've been given.

But every day God gives us small, endless blessings: sunshine and rain, flowers in the pavement, food and shelter, and family and friends. There's the encouragement that comes at just the right time, that verse that suddenly jumps off the page and straight into your heart, or the answered prayer. And then there is the greatest blessing of all: a God who loves you, walks with you, guides and guards you.

Now consider this beautiful thought: God has chosen each and every one of these blessings as a thoughtfully and intentionally chosen gift, just for you. Just because He loves you.

*Lord, I pray that today you would help me to see
all the blessings you have poured into my life. I
thank You, Lord, for each and every one. Amen.*

New Every Morning

The Lord's love never ends;
his mercies never stop.
They are new every morning . . .

LAMENTATIONS 3:22–23 NCV

It's the same old sin, that same one you've struggled with for so long. Every time you think you've mastered it, it creeps right back in, over and over again. You promise yourself you won't lash out in anger, or call that person, or watch that show. But here you are, on the other side of having done it yet again. Sorrow and regret keep you tossing and turning all through the night.

Take heart. You are not alone in your struggles. Paul confessed that "I do not understand what I do. For what I want to do I do not do, but what I hate I do" (Romans 7:15 NIV).

As you watch the sun rise and chase away the darkness, accept this truth: God's mercies are new each and every morning. So step out into the light of this new day and try again, trusting not in your own strength but in His—along with His mercy and grace.

*Lord, please give me the strength to conquer
the sin that plagues me. And please forgive
me for the times it conquers me. Amen.*

This Way

Your ears shall hear a word behind you,
saying, "This is the way, walk in it" . . .

ISAIAH 30:21 NKJV

Have you ever wondered how many decisions you make in a day? From the little things—what clothes to wear, what to have for breakfast, and which route to take to work—all the way up to which job you should take, which people you should surround yourself with, which doctor to see, or how to best help an aging parent. Some decisions have only a small impact on your life. Others loom so large and terrifying that they can leave you feeling breathless, helpless, and frozen.

Talk to God. And not just about the life-changing decisions but about the daily ones as well. Talk to Him, but don't end the conversation when you say "Amen." Stay connected to Him, listening for His guiding whisper: *This choice, not that one. This word, not that one. This way, not that way.* Trust God—not the world—and He will tell you the way you should go.

Lord, please guide me through the decisions
of this day and every day. And help me to
keep listening even after I say . . . Amen.

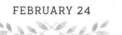

The Potter

> I went down to the potter's house, and I saw him working
> at the wheel. But the pot he was shaping from the clay
> was marred in his hands; so the potter formed it into
> another pot, shaping it as seemed best to him.
>
> JEREMIAH 18:3–4 NIV

The pot that the Heavenly Potter created was perfect until sin slipped in. Then it seemed ruined, damaged, and spoiled. "Throw it out!" the devil would say.

But not the Potter.

He lifts the pot gently back onto the wheel. With His own hands He shapes and smooths and gives that marred pot a new life and a new purpose.

You, dear friend, are the pot, and God is the Potter. You may think that your sins and mistakes make you unfit to serve Him—and the devil will certainly tell you the same. But don't listen to him. Give yourself over to the Potter, who will shape you and make you whole again.

*Lord, take me and make me into someone
who can be used by You. Amen.*

Whatever You Do

Whatever you do, work at it with all your heart, as
working for the Lord, not for human masters, since you
know that you will receive an inheritance from the Lord
as a reward. It is the Lord Christ you are serving.

COLOSSIANS 3:23–24 NIV

Whether it's preaching or praising; whether it's balancing the books or reading them to little ones; whether it's scrubbing for surgery or scrubbing the sink, give it your best. Put your heart into it. And not just to impress the boss or to please the other people in your life. Work as if you are working for the Lord, to impress and to please Him.

Why? Your works don't earn you a place in heaven, "for it is by grace you have been saved, through faith—and this is not from yourselves, it is the gift of God—not by works, so that no one can boast" (Ephesians 2:8–9 NIV). But isn't working hard the least you can do for the One Whose grace gives you salvation? As you go about your work today, in all its different forms, imagine you are working for God . . . because you always are.

Lord, when I'm frustrated by the work I need
to do, or tempted to do "just enough," remind
me that I'm really serving You. Help me to
put my heart into all I do today. Amen.

Be Good

The Lord is kind and merciful,
patient and full of love.
The Lord is good to everyone.
He shows his mercy to everything he made.

PSALM 145:8–9 ERV

*K*ind. Merciful. Patient. Full of love. This is who the Lord is. Not just for some people. Not just for those who never let a curse slip past their lips or a vengeful thought rattle through their minds. And not just for those who look and dress and talk like we do.

God is good to everyone, from the bad-tempered boss, to the homeless woman huddled on the park bench, to the rude teen on the subway. He looks at those people—at all people, including you—and He sees His wonderful creation. He gives us all His goodness.

So today, be good to everyone you encounter. Be like the Lord is to you.

Lord, help me look at the people I encounter today and see them the way You do—as Your wonderful and beloved creations. Amen.

What Does It Mean to Be Good?

Christ gave you an example to follow.

1 PETER 2:21 ERV

What does "being good" look like in today's world? Is it always smiling and being polite, and nice, and a bit like a cheerful Christian doormat?

Not at all. Being good doesn't mean always being pleasant. And it doesn't mean you happily take whatever this world wants to dish out. Take your cues from Jesus. What did He do?

Jesus told the truth, even when it wasn't what people wanted to hear—as with that rich young ruler who called Jesus "good" (Luke 18:18–25).

Jesus helped when He could, and He accepted when He couldn't—such as when He walked away from His own hometown (Luke 4:14–30). He prayed for those who hurt Him (Luke 23:34). And, most vitally of all, He obeyed His Father in everything—even in death (Matthew 26:39).

When you're not sure what "being good" means today, just look to Jesus. Do what He did.

Lord, please show me how to be good—and do good—
to those around me today. Just as You did. Amen.

A Place for You

"My Father's house has many rooms; if that were not so, would
I have told you that I am going there to prepare a place for
you? And if I go and prepare a place for you, I will come back
and take you to be with me that you also may be where I am."

JOHN 14:2–3 NIV

No room for you at the lunch table. No room for you in the
boardroom. No room for you in the club, the restaurant,
the plane . . . There are so many places in this world that refuse
to make room for you. And that stings, doesn't it?

Then let this truth sink deep into your heart: There is
room for you in heaven. And not just a space for you to slip
into unnoticed when no one is looking, but a room made spe-
cifically for you—carefully arranged, thoughtfully prepared by
Jesus Himself. And one day, when Jesus comes again, He will
take you to heaven, to the home He has built for you.

*Lord, when I start to feel as if there's no
place for me, remind me of the place You
have prepared just for me. Amen.*

MARCH

The Grace to Be Different

"John the Baptist did not go around eating and
drinking, and you said, 'John has a demon in him!'
But because the Son of Man goes around eating and
drinking, you say, 'Jesus eats and drinks too much!
He is even a friend of tax collectors and sinners.'"

LUKE 7:33–34 CEV

She dresses differently. His hair is different. They praise God differently. They sing *those* songs. They read *that* Bible. She prays this way, and he prays that way. He hangs out with those kinds of people, and she has a tattoo.

So what? In the eternal scheme of things, what does it matter? We humans have a knack for drawing lines—mostly lines that exclude. We even try to exclude others from the grace Jesus died to offer us. *All of us.*

The Pharisees gave Jesus so much grief because He didn't fit the mold of what they thought a follower of God should be. The fact is Jesus came to break the Pharisees' mold. Being a Christian isn't about being like everyone else; it's about being different from this world. It's about worshipping and following the One Who came to give us the grace to break the molds.

*Lord, forgive me for the times I judge others just
because they are different. Show me the lines I
have drawn and help me to erase them. Teach me
to offer grace to all, just as You did. Amen.*

Not Okay

The LORD himself goes before you and will be
with you; he will never leave you nor forsake you.
Do not be afraid; do not be discouraged.

DEUTERONOMY 31:8 NIV

There are days when you're just not okay. And you know what? That's okay.

It may just be all the little frustrations of life piling up: a leaking faucet, lost keys, lack of sleep. Or perhaps your world has been completely upended, and one of the "D's"—disaster, death, divorce—has descended upon you.

Jesus knows everything that you're dealing with, and He understands every frustration and every disaster. Remember that He walked this earth and lived this life, just as you do. Don't be afraid. Don't be discouraged. And don't throw in the towel. Jesus is walking right by your side. Lean into Him and His strength. Because it's okay to be not okay . . . but you don't have to stay that way.

*Jesus, I thank You for Your presence in
my life, for walking beside me. Please
lend me Your strength today. Amen.*

Soul Thirst

"Let anyone who is thirsty come to me and drink.
Whoever believes in me, as Scripture has said, rivers
of living water will flow from within them."

JOHN 7:37–38 NIV

Every soul is a thirsty soul. People try to quench that thirst with many different things. Some try the waters of this world: of busyness, money, and possessions. Others try the waters of relationships, expecting the people in their lives to fill their every need. Still others turn to the waters of sinful, harmful things. And while these things may quench their thirst for a moment or even longer, sooner or later the thirst returns stronger than ever.

There is only one way to quench that thirst within your soul: the Living Water of Jesus. For when you choose to follow Him, His own Spirit comes to live inside you, an ever-bubbling spring rising up within you. Only Jesus can truly quench the thirst of your soul, because, deep down, your soul has always been thirsting for Him.

*Lord, my soul thirsts for You. Fill me with Your
Living Water today and every day until it
overflows toward everyone around me. Amen.*

Tell God

I speak to God morning, noon, and night.
. . . [A]nd he listens to me!
PSALM 55:17 ERV

When you talk to God, it doesn't have to be during a major crisis or event. It doesn't have to be in a time of distress, big or frightening or life changing. Yes, of course God wants to hear from you in all those kinds of moments. He wants to help, to heal, and to guide you. But don't let those be the only times you talk to Him.

God wants in on all the little details of your life. The things that make you laugh and smile, the random thoughts that go zipping through your mind, the little frustrations that pepper your daily life—God wants to hear about them all. Why? Because He wants a *relationship* with you. An all-day, every day, anytime, good or bad, through-thick-and-thin relationship with you. Talk to Him today: He's waiting to hear from you.

Lord, it is so amazing to me that You want
to hear about all the little things that happen
in my life. Thank You for being a God
Who loves me enough to listen. Amen.

What Would Happen If . . .

"Then a despised Samaritan came along, and when he saw
the man, he felt compassion for him. Going over to him, the
Samaritan soothed his wounds with olive oil and wine and
bandaged them. Then he put the man on his own donkey
and took him to an inn, where he took care of him."

LUKE 10:33–34 NLT

What would happen if you really loved your neighbor?
If you gave love and comfort to those you were "supposed" to ignore or even hate?

The Samaritan man had every worldly reason to keep walking. The Jewish man lying on the ground wasn't someone he knew,
and his people were enemies; they had treated the Samaritan like
he was nothing better than dirt. The Samaritan had places to be
and things to accomplish. Why should he help this Jewish man?
Because that man was his neighbor. Everyone is our neighbor—
not the across-the-street kind, but the we-are-all-God's-beloved-
creations kind. And so the Samaritan loved his neighbor.

What would happen if you loved like that? You just might
change the world . . . or at least the world of that neighbor you
choose to love.

*Lord, is there a neighbor I need to love today? Guide
me to that person and give me the heart and the
courage to love them as You love me. Amen.*

Walking on Water

*When he saw the wind, he was afraid and, beginning
to sink, cried out, 'Lord, save me!' Immediately
Jesus reached out his hand and caught him.*

MATTHEW 14:30–31 NIV

There will be times when God asks you to walk on water—to do something that's utterly impossible for you. To forgive your enemy. To share His message with a certain person, or in a certain place. To speak His truth, to pray, to praise in the midst of a storm. You're convinced you'll flounder, drowning in the waves.

Trust Him. Step out of the boat and onto the water.

God is the One Who has the power. Jesus tells His disciples that "with man this is impossible, but with God all things are possible" (Matthew 19:26 NIV). And He will be right there beside you, enabling you to walk out onto shifting, uncertain territory. There's no need to be afraid. Even if you begin to sink, you need only call His name, and He is there *immediately*, reaching His hand down to you through the wind and the waves to lift you up to Him.

*Lord, sometimes the things You ask me to
do seem utterly impossible. But I will trust
You today—and every day. I will step out
of the boat and come to You. Amen.*

What You Can Do

"She did what she could."

MARK 14:8 NIV

So you haven't founded an orphanage for the poor and the abandoned. You haven't given up all your worldly possessions and become a missionary in an impoverished third-world country. You don't have a nationwide audience of millions hanging on your every word as you preach the gospel to them.

What can you do instead? You can hold the hand of a friend, listening and praying over her tears. You can teach a class of little ones. You can send a card, bake a cake, set up before, and clean up after. Behind the scenes or out in front for all to see, you can do what you can do for God. He will see, He will smile, and He will remember . . . *She did what she could.*

Be faithful in the place God has planted you, with the task God has given you. And that, sweet child, will be enough for God.

Lord, I sometimes feel that I don't do enough for You—because it's not huge and grand. Show me the task You have for me today, and help me to do what I can do. Amen.

Fly Away

*Oh, I wish I had wings like a dove. I would
fly away and find a place to rest.*

PSALM 55:6 ERV

Have you ever felt envious of a bird in flight? How wonderful would it be to just spread your wings and fly away from all your troubles? From the deadlines and the drudgery, the endless and mindless tasks, the gossips, the backstabbers, and the downright mean. That's certainly what David was thinking when he penned this psalm.

God knows you need a place of peace far away from the noise and clamor of this world. That's why He gives you *Himself*. Turn to Him, morning, noon, and night. Tell Him what is upsetting you. "He listens to me!" (Psalm 55:17 ERV), "he will care for you" (Psalm 55:22 ERV), and "[He] will give you rest" (Matthew 11:28 NIV).

Close your eyes. Let your thoughts fly away to God. His grace will give you a place for you to rest.

*Holy Father, I praise You for being a God Who
listens, Who cares, and Who gives me rest. Amen.*

One Way

*"I am the way, the truth, and the life. No one
comes to the Father except through Me."*

JOHN 14:6 NKJV

There are probably a dozen different ways to get to the other side of your town. There are at least a hundred different ways to get to the other side of the country. In fact, there are millions of different ways to reach a million different places. But there is only one way to get to the Father.

Jesus is the door into heaven (John 10:9), and "salvation is found in no one else" (Acts 4:12 NIV). This world will tell you that all paths lead to God. It's a beautiful thought, but it's a lie. No one comes to the Father except through Jesus. Love Him, follow Him, obey Him (John 14:15). And His grace will carry you home to heaven with Him (John 14:3).

*Lord Jesus, You are the only way to God.
And I praise You for making a way—the
way—to heaven for me. Amen.*

Who You Are

See what great love the Father has lavished on us, that we should be called children of God! And that is what we are!

1 JOHN 3:1 NIV

Think for a moment about all the different names we give ourselves. There are names that define our relationships: "husband," "wife," "mother," "daughter," "sister," "brother," "friend." There are the names that explain our place in this world: "banker," "lawyer," "stay-at-home mom," "teacher," "writer." And then there are those names we call ourselves in our darkest moments: "coward," "loser," "unworthy."

There is a lot of power in a name. So today put aside all those other names—especially the darkest ones—and call yourself by your one true name. The one that defines your most important relationship. The one that tells the world who you really are. The one that the God of All Creation, in His lavish love, bestowed upon you: "child of God." For that is who you truly are.

Lord, help me to set aside whatever name this world or my own thoughts are tempted to call me. I know my true name is "child of God." Amen.

Get a Little Dirty

Humble yourselves in the sight of the
Lord, and He will lift you up.

JAMES 4:10 NKJV

Jesus didn't mind kneeling in the dirt to scratch out words while He waited for a bunch of Pharisees to drop their stones and let a woman go free. He didn't mind touching blind beggars, dusty from the streets, or lepers, contagious and "unclean." And He didn't mind stooping to wash the dirt from the feet of the men who would soon run away from Him.

Jesus wasn't afraid to get a little dirty. But are you? Because this world is full of dirt—dirt on people, dirt in lives, and dirt within ourselves. And Jesus could use some followers who aren't afraid to get a little dirty. How can you serve Jesus this way today?

Lord, forgive me for turning away
from the dusty and dirty of this world. I
know that You never did. Amen.

Undeserved Kindness

By faith we have been made acceptable to God. And now,
because of our Lord Jesus Christ, we live at peace with God.
Christ has also introduced us to God's undeserved kindness . . .

ROMANS 5:1–2 CEV

God gives you grace so abundantly, an undeserved kindness that you could never earn. But do you give that same undeserved kindness to the people who wrong you?

From the heavy betrayals like the parent who abandoned you, the friend who broke your heart, or the spouse who lied to you, to the everyday stuff like the guy who cuts you off in traffic or the waiter who seems to intentionally keep you waiting . . . do you seek revenge, to get even, or to get back at them? Or do you give the undeserved kindness of grace?

You know what God did—and continues to do for you. Do the same, even when it's difficult—especially then. Give the undeserved kindness of grace to someone in your life today.

Lord, forgive me for all the times I claim Your grace
but then refuse to give it to others. Help me to offer
the undeserved kindness of grace today. Amen.

Sunshine and Rain

> "'Be not dismayed, for I *am* your God.
> I will strengthen you,
> Yes, I will help you,
> I will uphold you with My righteous right hand.'"
>
> ISAIAH 41:10 NKJV

Some days it's easy to be grateful—when the blessings are often and obvious. When it could only have been God who solved the unsolvable. Even just a day flooded with the "ordinary" blessings of a new sunrise, a loved one to hug, and raindrops to wash the world can stir up feelings of gratitude.

But there are days when it's harder to be grateful, when we begin to question God's goodness. Because the bad guys have won, because the relationship is still lost, because rain was just the last straw in a washed-up day.

You might find yourself asking, *Where is God in all this?* Look closer. He's right beside you, holding fast to you and saying, *I've got you. And it's going to be better than okay.* So lift up your praises to God—in the sunshine and in the rain. God will never stop being good, so don't ever stop being grateful.

Lord, I will praise You—in sunshine and rain, when I see Your blessings and when I don't. I know You are holding fast to me with Your own hand. Amen.

Like Him

"If you have seen me, you have seen the Father."

JOHN 14:8–9 CEV

Have you ever wondered what God looks like? For Jacob, He was a stranger wrestling in the darkness (Genesis 32). For Moses, He was a flaming bush that did not burn (Exodus 3). For Elijah, He was a whisper after the wind, the earthquake, and fire (1 Kings 19).

But what does God really look like? Jesus gave us the answer: God looks like Him. The God of the universe put on Jesus's eyes, and His nose, and His dark hair and skin. He became fully human in order to enter into our world, but in His heart He was still fully divine. God looks like Jesus.

God looks like grace.

Lord, as much as I would love to see Your face, I know I have seen Your heart—in the life and love and grace of Jesus. Amen.

When We Are Weak

But he said to me, "My grace is enough for you, for
my power is made perfect in weakness." So then,
I will boast most gladly about my weaknesses, so
that the power of Christ may reside in me.

2 CORINTHIANS 12:9 NET

Satan is forever trying to extinguish the work of grace within
our hearts with troubles, with distractions, and with everyday annoyances. Anything that might take our focus off Jesus
or cause us to doubt His power—that is what Satan will throw
at us. And when we are at our weakest, that's when he most
likes to strike. When we're tired, or overwhelmed, or still reeling from the latest in a line of disasters.

But when we are at our weakest, that's also when Christ's
power within us can be the strongest. As we lean into Him,
emptied of all our own resources, He fills us to overflowing
with His own strength. To sustain us, yes, but more impor-
tantly to proclaim to us that we can overcome our struggles
through His grace and power alone.

*Lord, You never run out of power or grace,
but I so often do. When I am empty, remind
me to turn to You to be filled. Amen.*

Come Away and Rest

*"Come with me by yourselves to a quiet
place and get some rest."*

MARK 6:31 NIV

Jesus's disciples were exhausted. Exhausted by their own efforts and by the news of John the Baptist's death. They were physically, emotionally, and spiritually beat-up. They needed to rest. And that's just what Jesus told them to do. Not just to sleep, but to come away with Him, alone, "to a quiet place."

Why has "rest" become such an ugly word in our world? Why have we allowed the rush and push and pull of busyness to steal it away from us? Rest is not only a physical need; it's mental and emotional as well. It's why God rested on the seventh day; it's why He gave us a Sabbath. So listen to Jesus as He gently commands you to come away with Him and rest in His arms.

*Lord, why is it so hard for me to simply step
away and rest? Help me lay everything down
and find true rest in Your presence. Amen.*

Chosen

You are a chosen people, royal priests, a holy nation,
a people for God's own possession. You were chosen
to tell about the wonderful acts of God, who called
you out of darkness into his wonderful light.

1 PETER 2:9 NCV

How do you see yourself? Good-looking or not so beautiful? Capable or incompetent? Strong or weak? No one important or a child of the Most High King?

Now how do you think God sees you? Maybe you aren't so sure. Pick up the mirror of God—His Word—and let Him show you the image of who you really are.

You have been chosen by God, adopted into His royal family. You have been made holy by the blood of Christ. You are God's own special and beloved possession. And He has given you a job to do: to tell the world about all the wonderful things He has done, that He wants each and every person to be His chosen one. Who can you tell today?

*Holy Father, thank You for making me Your chosen
and adopted child. I pray that You will guide me
today to someone I can tell about You. Amen.*

Worry: The Enemy

My God will meet all your needs according to
the riches of his glory in Christ Jesus.

PHILIPPIANS 4:19 NIV

It has been said that worry is the enemy of faith. Think about that one for a moment: God has promised to give you everything you need. So if we believe that God will do what He has promised, then why do we worry? Do we truly believe that God will do what He has said He will do?

Some people will even tell you that worry is a sin—which just gives you one more thing to worry about! But worry is actually more of a sign—a sign that you have forgotten who your God is. He is all-knowing and all-powerful, so He knows exactly what you need and is able to deliver it. But more than that, God is infinitely loving. He will deliver what you need in the way that is best for you eternally.

*Lord, worry seems to sneak up on me, usually
when I take my eyes off You. Help me to keep my
eyes—and my faith—firmly fixed on You. Amen.*

Listen to Others

Everyone should be quick to listen, slow to speak . . .

JAMES 1:19 NIV

B eing a listener is a rare skill to have—or at least a rare skill to practice. Perhaps this is because it takes time, and we're always in such a hurry. And perhaps because it takes selflessness, and we tend to be a bit selfish, don't we?

The next time someone is trying to talk to you—really talk to you—make a decided effort to listen. Give that person your full attention. Don't be so quick to jump in with your own story or opinion. Don't be a fix-it-all, know-it-all, or judge-of-all. Just lean in and listen. It's a gift you can give to those in your life, a beautiful and necessary kind of grace.

*Lord, teach me to listen to others and, in my listening,
to always point them back to You. Amen.*

Listen to God

> "My sheep listen to my voice; I know
> them, and they follow me."
>
> JOHN 10:27 NLT

As important as it is to listen to others, it is even more important to be still, cast up your heart in prayer, and listen to God.

How often—or how seldom—do we really do this? Instead, we usually come and kneel before Him . . . and do all of the talking ourselves, as if we were the ones who had the answers. How often must God long to lean down from His throne, place a finger upon our lips, and whisper, *Shhh! Child, listen to Me?*

So today, go and kneel before Him, little lamb. Open your ears, your heart, your soul—but not your mouth—and simply listen as the Shepherd speaks to you.

Lord, I come before You now to listen. . . . Amen.

Remember

God, in your Temple, we remember your loving kindness.

PSALM 48:9 ERV

Do you remember God's loving-kindness? Whether it's stepping into the temple of His church or the temple of your own heart where His Spirit resides (1 Corinthians 3:16), do you remember the ways that God has shown His love and grace to you?

It's so easy to step into His presence and lay out your list of worries, requests, or even demands. And you should certainly pour your heart out before Him. But don't forget to remember His goodness too. Delight in the sheer wonder of Who God is in this world and in your life. Consider all He has done for you, all the grace He has rained down upon you—and rejoice! *Remember* God's loving-kindness in your life—and praise Him as you step into His presence.

Holy Father and Mighty God, I praise You for all the wonders You have done. There is no other God like You! Amen.

Sit with Him

They went to a place called Gethsemane, and Jesus
said to his disciples, "Sit here while I pray."

MARK 14:32 NIV

"Sit here while I pray." That's all Jesus asked His disciples to do, but even that proved to be a struggle. It's not easy for us to simply sit with Jesus, even when—or perhaps especially when—life seems to be in its darkest hours. When we feel completely helpless, we think we need to be up and out and doing something. It makes us feel like we're accomplishing something.

But the best place to be is at the feet of Jesus while He offers up prayers to His Father on our behalf (1 John 2:1). When life throws everything it has at you—from mounting bills to dreaded diagnoses to the everyday exhaustion of life—obey Your Savior. Simply be in His presence, and sit here while He prays for you.

*Lord Jesus, I am so humbled by the fact that
You choose to pray for me. Cover me with
Your prayers and Your grace. Amen.*

Run to Him

Then all of Jesus' followers left him and ran away.

MARK 14:50 NCV

This couldn't possibly be right. This couldn't possibly be the way things are supposed to happen. Those were probably some of the thoughts going through the disciples' heads as they ran away from Jesus that night in the garden. Their Savior had been arrested, and everything they thought they understood about Him and His plan was suddenly destroyed.

Have you ever thought those same thoughts? Have you ever been following what you *thought* was Your Savior's plan and then suddenly found yourself in your own Garden of Gethsemane, questioning everything you believed was true?

When everything you thought you understood about Jesus turns out to be outside His plan, don't run away from Him. Run *to* Him. Because His plan is so much greater than you can ever understand.

Lord, there is so much about You and Your plans that doesn't make sense to me. Help me to hold fast to You, especially when I don't understand. Amen.

The Trial

*If anyone does sin, we have an advocate who
pleads our case before the Father. He is Jesus
Christ, the one who is truly righteous.*

1 JOHN 2:1 NLT

It was a mockery of a trial. The outcome had been decided before it even began. Rules were broken, witnesses lied, and accusations flew from every side. There was no justice here and no defense was offered, only scorn, contempt, and condemning judgment.

It was the trial of Jesus, our Lord.

You have a trial coming too, a judgment day. And the devil would love to make sure it goes much the way Jesus's did. This is why Jesus died—and rose: so that your judgment day will be very different from His. Yes, the devil will accuse you (Revelation 12:10). He won't even have to lie, because we all know the wrongs that we have done. And he'll demand that a price be paid for your sins. But you have a defender—*the* Defender. Jesus steps before God the Judge and says, "This one is Mine. The price has already been paid."

*Lord Jesus, thank You for defending me from
the evil one's accusations and for paying the
price so that I can be set free. Amen.*

Crown for a Crown

They stripped him and put a scarlet robe on him, and then twisted together a crown of thorns and set it on his head.

MATTHEW 27:28–29 NIV

On the cross, Jesus wore a crown of thorns. It should have been ours. Everything He suffered—the arrest, the beatings, the cross—should have been ours. Because Jesus didn't sin—we did. We are the guilty ones.

Jesus took on the punishment that should have been ours. That is His mercy. In return, He gave us His own righteousness. That is His grace. And together, mercy and grace become our salvation.

Jesus didn't come to carry out the justice of the Law. He came to make a trade with us—a crown for a crown. On the cross, Jesus wore *our* crown of thorns so that we could wear *His* crown of righteousness (2 Timothy 4:8). Jesus isn't about eye-for-an-eye justice; instead, He offers us crown-for-a-crown grace.

Lord Jesus, it should have been me. Let my life today be a living praise for Your crown-for-a-crown grace. Amen.

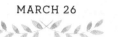

The Same God

When I look at the night sky and see
the work of your fingers—
the moon and the stars you set in place—
what are mere mortals that you should think about them,
human beings that you should care for them?
PSALM 8:3–4 NLT

When night falls, step outside, look up into the heavens, and imagine. Imagine the might it took to not only create that moon but to hang it in space and hold it there. Imagine the meticulous planning and understanding it took to establish universes, orbits, and rotations. *That* is the power of God.

Now imagine a Man, so beaten and so bloody He no longer seems a man. Imagine nails piercing hands and feet. Imagine the darkness descending, the ground trembling, and the Voice crying out, "Father, forgive them, for they do not know what they do" (Luke 23:34 NKJV). *That* is also the power of God.

The same Lord who stretched out His hands to set the moon and the stars in their places also stretched out His hands on the splinter-roughened wood of a Roman cross for you—to give you grace.

Lord, I look up into the heavens, at the wonders
You created, and I am amazed. But I am even
more amazed by the grace You purchased for me
on that cross. Thank You, O my Lord. Amen.

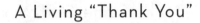

A Living "Thank You"

Those who passed by hurled insults at him, shaking their
heads and saying, "You who are going to destroy the
temple and build it in three days, save yourself! Come
down from the cross, if you are the Son of God!"

MATTHEW 27:39–40 NIV

Jesus could have stepped down off that cross Himself. He
could have called the armies of heaven's angels to destroy
those who sought to destroy Him. He could have simply walked
away and left us to simmer in our sins.

But He didn't. Jesus chose not to help Himself so that He
could help you. He gave Himself no mercy so that He could
give you endless grace.

Jesus gave you—gave each of us who are willing to love
and follow Him—a priceless gift, one we can never, ever repay
Him. So shouldn't our lives be a living "Thank You" to Him?

*Lord, words could never say how grateful I am
for Your grace. But I pray that You will help me
make my life a living "Thank You" to You. Show
me how to show my gratefulness today. Amen.*

Turned Away

And at the ninth hour Jesus cried out with a loud voice,
saying, "Eloi, Eloi, lama sabachthani?" which is translated,
"My God, My God, why have You forsaken Me?"

MARK 15:34 NKJV

In the most heartbreaking moment in all of eternity, God turned away from His Son. And the Son, who had never for an instant in all of eternity been separated from His Father, was alone on the cross. His anguished cry still echoes, even after all these years.

Jesus took all the sins of all the world upon Himself and took the punishment for them—our punishment. And God, in His perfect holiness, had to turn away. That moment changed your eternity. Jesus took your place so that you could take His—as a perfect, sinless lamb of God.

God turned away from Jesus so that He never has to turn away from you. That is His greatest gift. That is His grace.

Holy Father, how could my words ever say what
needs to be said? I'm sorry my sins needed such a
sacrifice. I'm sorry to have caused You such sorrow.
But I thank You, Lord, for Your grace. Amen.

It Is Finished

*Jesus said, "It is finished." With that, he
bowed his head and gave up his spirit.*

JOHN 19:30 NIV

Jesus had finished what He came to do.

The Son of God stepped down from heaven, cloaked Himself in the body of a man, and walked among His people. He did it to be a living example for us, to show us how to love the Father and how to live as God's people. But more than that, Jesus came to die.

Jesus allowed Himself to be arrested, beaten, mocked, and tried. He allowed Roman hands to nail His body to a rough wooden cross. He allowed Himself to suffer for all the world's sins. And before He died, He said, "It is finished." The power of sin to condemn His people was broken. Its grip on us was finished forever. But the grace of God had only just begun.

*Holy Lord Jesus, I do not have the words to praise
You for the price You paid to set me free from sin.
So I give You my life. Use me, Lord Jesus. Amen.*

Would You?

Christ died for the ungodly.
ROMANS 5:6 NIV

Would you die for the "ungodly"? Would you die for that person who left when you needed them most, or the person you trusted with your confidences only to find your secrets shared with the world? Would you die for the adulterers, the gossips, the liars, the murderers—and worse!—of this world?

Christ did.

Look at the magnitude of grace contained in these few words: "Very rarely will anyone die for a righteous person, though for a good person someone might possibly dare to die. But God demonstrates his own love for us in this: While we were still sinners, Christ died for us" (Romans 5:7–8 NIV). Few people would die to save the wretches of the world, but Christ did. He died for all the sinners. He died for you. Why? Because that's how God has shown us His love—His incredible, amazing grace.

Holy Father, I come to You now. I don't have it all together or all figured out. I'm still a sinner. But I'm a sinner who is so very thankful for Your amazing grace. Amen.

The Grace of a Borrowed Tomb

Joseph took the body, wrapped it in a clean linen cloth, and placed it in his own new tomb that he had cut out of the rock.

MATTHEW 27:59–60 NIV

The Son of Man had "no place to lay his head"—not even in death (Luke 9:58 NIV). He was born in a stable to a poor peasant girl, a craftsman's son—not a king's. There was no royal crown, no golden riches, no palaces.

What does all that tell you about the value Jesus placed on the things of this world? And what does it tell you about the value *you* should place on the things of this world? You see, nothing in this world is worth as much to Jesus as the riches He found in saving you.

As you walk through your day today—as all the "stuff" of this world beckons to you—remember that borrowed tomb and the grace it gives to you.

Holy Father, help me this day to see the true value of the things of this world and the true value of You. Amen.

APRIL

Immovable Stones

> On their way, they were asking one another, "Who
> will roll the stone away from the entrance for us?"
>
> MARK 16:3 CEV

The women made their way to the tomb of Jesus in the early morning stillness. As they walked, they realized there was a problem with their plan. *The stone.* That massive stone that sealed Jesus's tomb was just too big for them to move themselves. Who would roll it away for them? You know the story, of course. When they reached the tomb, God himself had already moved the stone.

How often do you try to move your own immovable stones? Like the stone of your sins that keeps you trapped in a spiritual grave. That's a stone only God can move for you— and the wonderful news is that He already has.

*Thank You, Holy Father, for that rolled-away
stone and that empty tomb. And thank You for
rolling away the stone of my sins. Amen.*

Beautifully Empty

The angel told the women, "Don't be afraid, because I know you are looking for Jesus who was crucified. He is not here. For he has risen, just as he said. Come and see the place where he lay."

MATTHEW 28:5–6 CSB

Emptiness is usually seen as a bad thing: empty pockets, empty bank accounts, empty refrigerator. Sometimes this emptiness can refer to us as well: empty hearts, empty hope, or an empty life.

But Jesus came, and died, and rose to life again to leave behind an empty tomb. And then emptiness became a wonderful thing. "Do not worry, saying 'What shall we eat?' or 'What shall we drink?' or 'What shall we wear?'" Jesus tells us (Matthew 6:31 NIV). Because of that empty tomb, your empty pockets and bank accounts and refrigerators can be entrusted to a God who promises to care for you. Your empty heart can be filled with love, your empty hope filled with the promise of heaven, and your empty life filled—to overflowing—with the power of God at work in you.

All because of an empty tomb.

Lord Jesus, I pray that the beautiful emptiness of that tomb and all it promises will fill my heart and life to overflowing with You. Amen.

Included

"Now go and tell his disciples, including Peter, that
Jesus is going ahead of you to Galilee. You will see
him there, just as he told you before he died.

MARK 16:7 NLT

The angel stood by the empty tomb—the one that could
not hold the Savior. He had a message for the women to
deliver. "Go and tell his disciples, including Peter . . ."

Including Peter.

The same Peter who had run away from Jesus in the garden. The same Peter who had slunk back to listen outside His
trial. And the same Peter who had said not once, not twice, but
three times that he didn't even know this man called Jesus. The
same Peter who broke down and wept when he realized what
he'd done.

The Lord made sure that the message the angel delivered
mentioned Peter by name—who no doubt wondered if Jesus's
love and grace still included Him. It did. And when you make
mistakes—even ones that seem unforgivable—grace still includes you too.

*Lord, thank You for a love and grace so perfect and
so far-reaching that it includes even me. Amen.*

The Foolishness of Grace

The message of the cross is foolishness to those who are perishing, but to us who are being saved it is the power of God.

1 CORINTHIANS 1:18 NIV

It doesn't sound like the ideal plan, does it? Send Your one and only Son from heaven to be born in the dirt and poverty of the earth. Allow Him to be humbled, humiliated, and crucified. Turn away from Him as He—Who never sinned—takes upon Himself the sins of all the world. Watch as He is buried in a borrowed tomb, and then three days later raise Him to life again. Yet that was God's plan. *God's perfect plan.*

It might not be logical to us. There are even those who would dare to say it was foolish. But for those of us who believe, who know how much we've been forgiven, who know the depths of sin from which God has saved us, it is grace . . . *beautiful grace.*

Lord, Your ways are so much greater than I can understand. But I am so grateful for the salvation You've given me through Your perfect plan. Amen.

The Why

"I, even I, am he who blots out
your transgressions, for my own sake,
and remembers your sins no more."

ISAIAH 43:25 NIV

God did it all—sent His Son from the throne room of heaven, watched Him be born and live and die—for us. Because His love for us is so great, He sent Jesus to save us from the sins that would condemn us. That's the promise of John 3:16. But that's only part of the story—the *what*. The rest—the *why*—is wrapped up in four little words:

For my own sake.

God loves you so much that to be separated from you for all eternity would break His heart. So He made a way for you to be with Him. God longs to blot out your transgressions, to remember your sins no more. For you, yes. But He also gives you His grace for His own sake.

Holy Father, this love and grace You offer is so
great I cannot comprehend it. But I wrap myself in
it—and offer my own love back to You. Amen.

Someday

> At the name of Jesus every knee should bow, of those
> in heaven, and of those on earth, and of those under
> the earth, and *that* every tongue should confess that
> Jesus Christ *is* Lord, to the glory of God the Father.
>
> PHILIPPIANS 2:10–11 NKJV

I t's hurtful to see the way this world treats our Savior, joking and laughing and mocking. At best, people might call Him a good man or a teacher. But more often, they'll declare He's nothing more than a fable for people to cling to.

But Jesus wasn't just a good man or a teacher, and He's certainly no fairy tale. He lived here on this earth for over thirty years. He is the Son of God. He is our Savior.

More than that, He is Lord, and one day no one will be able to deny that. One day He will return, just as He promised. And on that day every knee will bow and every tongue will confess Who He really is.

Let one day be today for you.

Lord Jesus, I kneel before you now and
I confess—You are Lord! Amen.

The Lord Is with You

"The LORD your God is with you wherever you go."

JOSHUA 1:9 NKJV

The Lord is with you.

He doesn't have to be, you know. He could have said, "I created an amazing world for you: Go live in it." He could have said, "I gave you the Bible filled with instructions on how to live: Go do what it says." He could have said, "You just keep choosing the wrong things—sometimes deliberately. I'm washing My hands of you."

But God didn't say any of those things. He didn't leave us or give up on us. Instead, He has promised to be with us, wherever we go, every step of the way. He sent us His Son so we would never be alone; and then, after Jesus left, He sent us His Spirit (John 16:7).

Today, every time you take a step, remember that God is right there beside you, keeping His promise forever.

Holy Father, I praise You for Your presence in my life. To know that I never have to face this world on my own is one of Your most precious gifts. Amen.

Guard Your Heart

Above all else, guard your heart,
for everything you do flows from it.

PROVERBS 4:23 NIV

I t's easy to look at this verse and think you should guard your heart by locking it away from the world. We want to protect our own hearts, especially if we've been hurt—and who among us hasn't?

But when God tells you to guard your heart, He isn't telling you to close it off. It's actually just the opposite. When we open our hearts, we let love pour out toward the people and the world. We let others see what loving God and loving others looks like as we live it out in our own lives.

Open your heart and let the love pour out, but . . . guard your heart and be careful of what you allow the world to pour *into* it. We can guard our hearts from hate, unkindness, and selfishness with prayer, with God's wisdom, and with God's Word.

Guard your heart well as you open it in love.

Lord, teach me to open my heart to love others while
also guarding my heart from those people and things
who would pull me away from You. Amen.

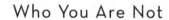

Who You Are Not

There is one Lord, one faith, one baptism,
one God and Father of all,
who is over all, in all, and living through all.

EPHESIANS 4:5–6 NLT

There is great grace in knowing who you are: a wonderfully and marvelously made child of God (Psalm 139:14; 1 John 3:1). But there is also great grace in knowing who you are not: God Himself.

You don't have to do it all or know it all. You don't have to have it all squared away or all figured out. You don't have to control all the details or have all the control. You don't have to *be* it all, because God is. God is all-knowing and all-powerful. He is Lord over all—details great and small.

And isn't that such a sweet and blessed relief? Today you can surrender your all to God and His sweet, blessed grace.

Lord, I give You my all—my life, my heart, my soul. Take control. Amen.

It Takes Courage

*Be kind to one another, tenderhearted, forgiving
one another, even as God in Christ forgave you.*

EPHESIANS 4:32 NKJV

It takes courage to be kind, especially when you suspect that your kindness may not be noticed, accepted, or returned. We may never receive a tangible reward for our kindness; we should be courageous with it anyway.

Be kind in little ways. Hold the door for others. Wave when someone lets you merge in front of them in traffic. Add an extra dollar or two to the tip. Even a small kindness might brighten someone's dark day in ways you can't imagine.

And be kind—courageously kind—in big ways. Invite that grouchy neighbor over for dinner. Send the card to that relative who pulled away. Offer to pray for that now-struggling coworker who gossiped about you.

Love your neighbor. Forgive others. Pray for your enemy. They may never notice or care, but it's what Jesus would do. And your courageous kindness just might soften someone's hardened heart.

*Lord, show me ways that I can be kind—
courageously kind—to others today. Amen.*

Always

[God] has always rescued me . . .
PSALM 55:18 ERV

David knew the meaning of "always," because he was a man who often needed rescuing. Rescue from his enemies, rescue from betrayal, and, as often as not, rescue from himself. Because, let's face it, David made some pretty massive mistakes in the course of his life.

David's mistakes gave him sorrow and pain, but they should give us hope. Because God *did* rescue David from his enemies, from those who betrayed him, and from his own sins. Let that truth give you hope today, because God will also rescue you. *Always.*

Lord, You rescue me in every way possible. Teach me to be a person after Your own heart. Amen.

A Drizzly Day

Wash away all my iniquity
and cleanse me from my sin.

PSALM 51:2 NIV

Some days are neither rain nor shine; they're simply gray and drizzly. And some people will tell you that these sorts of days are dreary and depressing. But what if you chose to see the drizzly days for the beauty they have instead of the beauty they lack?

Notice how the shimmer of raindrops makes the greens of the leaves more vibrant, as if they're sprinkled with countless tiny diamonds. Let those raindrops remind you of the countless tiny graces of God that cover the dreary drizzle of your sins and mistakes so that you shimmer like a beautiful and precious, grace-encrusted diamond.

Wash me, Lord. Cleanse me of all my sins
and cover me with Your grace. Amen.

Grace When We Fall

> When [the devil] lies, he speaks his native
> language, for he is a liar and the father of lies.
>
> JOHN 8:44 NIV

The devil is a liar. He has been lying from the very beginning, so he's had a lot of practice, which means he's very good at it. It also means that sometimes you'll fall for his lies. You'll believe him when he whispers that that particular sin isn't really all that sinful. You'll follow along when he says, "Everyone else is acting this way, so it must be okay." You'll see the pretty temptation instead of the terrible trap.

But then the time will come when—like Adam and Eve hiding in the garden—you realize what you have done. You fell for his lies. And although it's tempting, don't try to hide from God. Instead, run and tell everything to your Savior. Fall at His feet, and then let Him lift you up with His truth. Because there is grace—even when you fall for the lies.

*Lord, if any of the devil's lies are working in my life
today, replace them with Your truth. And please
forgive me for the times when I fall. Amen.*

What to Do?

If any of you need wisdom, you should ask God, and it will be given to you. God is generous and won't correct you for asking.

JAMES 1:5 CEV

What should you do when you don't know what to do? Ask God.

God doesn't just leave us to muddle through life and its many choices all on our own. Instead, He gives us anytime, anywhere access to His perfect wisdom; all we have to do is ask Him for it. It's one of His promises.

Sometimes God will show you the path to take in flashing-neon-billboard style. Other times He'll show you only the next step to take—or the one *not* to take—and then He'll ask you to trust Him to show the one after that. Sometimes you just have to walk in His ways, according to His teachings, as the path becomes clear to you.

Today, if you don't know what to do, ask God. He won't scold you for not already knowing the answer. In fact, He'll gift you with His wisdom, and He'll love the fact that you turned to Him.

Lord, guide me this day and every day with Your perfect wisdom. Show me the path to take—and the ones not to take. Amen.

Give Yourself to God

"Give to Caesar what belongs to Caesar, and give to God what belongs to God."

<small>MATTHEW 22:21 NLT</small>

The Pharisees were up to their old tricks. They asked Jesus if it was lawful to pay taxes to Caesar, who considered himself to be a god. If Jesus said yes, they could accuse Him of worshipping other gods. If He said no, they could accuse Him of rebellion. It was a perfect trap—or so they thought. But Jesus reminded them of this truth: The coin was stamped with Caesar's image, so give it to Caesar. Then He added, "Give to God what belongs to God."

What belongs to God? Where is His image stamped? The answer is all the way back in Genesis 1:27: "So God created mankind in his own image . . ." (NIV). *You* are stamped with God's image. Give yourself to God—heart, mind, body, and soul—because you belong to Him.

Holy Father, never let me forget Whom I belong to. May my words, my actions, and my giving always be pleasing to You. Amen.

Someone

*In whatever you do, don't let selfishness or pride be your
guide. Be humble, and honor others more than yourselves.*

<small>PHILIPPIANS 2:3 ERV</small>

Your Sunday school class just had the most wonderful
lunch, but now someone needs to stay and clean up the
mess. There are dishes to be washed and trash to be taken out.
But someone will take care of that, right? After all, you've had
such a long week. . . .

Someone needs to sort through all those donations and see
what's actually usable. But those bags smell a little funny . . .

Someone needs to stay in the nursery, drive the car, help
the hurting friend, and serve the meals . . . but you're *someone*.

You are the someone who can wash dishes, take out trash,
or do whatever is needed. Because, after all, why shouldn't
someone be *you*?

*Lord, forgive me for not being willing to do
the less-than-glamorous things that need doing.
Help me to be that someone today. Amen.*

The Image of God

Love and faithfulness meet together;
righteousness and peace kiss each other.

PSALM 85:10 NIV

We cannot see the face of God—at least, not on this side of heaven. And while we can't imagine Him with our own eyes, we can see His image with our hearts and minds.

God is the meeting of love and faithfulness. He is perfect and unconditional love, love that never ends or wavers (Lamentations 3:22–23). And He offers us a faithfulness that never falters. He keeps every promise He makes to us, even when we don't keep our promises to Him; "If we are faithless, he remains faithful, for he cannot disown himself" (2 Timothy 2:13 NIV).

What does God look like? Close your eyes and open your heart. You'll find His image where perfect love and unending faithfulness meet.

Lord, help me to see You today. I want to see the
image of Your perfect love and faithfulness—
and to reflect it back to You. Amen.

Shelter, Shield, and Protect

The Lord says, "If someone trusts me, I will save them.
I will protect my followers who call to me for help."

PSALM 91:14 ERV

When you find yourself stuck in the middle of a battle—at work, at home, in a relationship, or in church—you might find yourself wondering just exactly what God's saving and protection actually look like. Psalm 91 gives the answer: If we trust God, He will save us. If we call to Him for help, He will protect us.

God provides us a fortress to hide in (Psalm 91:2). He covers and shelters us, like a bird spreading her wings over her young (Psalm 91:4). He shields us from the enemy's arrows (Psalm 91:4–5). And He sends His angels to protect us wherever we go (Psalm 91:11).

So whatever battles come today—whether big or small—remember that God is your fortress, and He promises to shelter, shield, and protect you.

*When troubles come, Lord, please help
me remember to run to You for protection.
Cover me and shield me. Amen.*

Even If

His unfailing love toward those who fear him
is as great as the height of the heavens above the earth.
He has removed our sins as far from us
as the east is from the west.

<small>PSALM 103:11–12 NLT</small>

You messed up. You didn't mean to, but it happened. Or maybe you knew it was wrong, but you squared your shoulders, jutted out your chin, and charged right into that sin. You thought the thought, said the words, did the deeds, or continued that relationship. You did the very thing you knew God didn't want you to do.

Then you realize what you've done. And even though you know His promised grace is still for you, you can't seem to stop yourself from wondering: *Could God still love and forgive me, even after this?*

Hear this, dear heart: He can, He does, and He will. God's love and grace are still for you. Even if.

Lord, I'm so sorry . . . again. Please forgive and give
me the strength to remove this sin from my life. Amen.

Unclean

A leper came and worshiped Him, saying, "Lord,
if You are willing, You can make me clean."
Then Jesus put out His hand and touched him, saying, "I am
willing; be cleansed." Immediately his leprosy was cleansed.

MATTHEW 8:2–3 NKJV

"Unclean! Unclean!" The word defined the leper's day, his night, every moment of his life.

He wasn't allowed to work or to be with his family and friends. He was not even allowed to worship. People refused to look at him, and children ran away in fear as he called out, "Unclean! Unclean!" But Jesus didn't run away. He looked at him with love in His eyes, not loathing. His reached out to touch and heal and make him clean.

Think about the thing you're most ashamed of. We all have the something that makes our hearts call out, *Unclean! Unclean!* But Jesus won't run away. He looks at you with love, not loathing. He's reaching out to you. Let Him touch you, heal you, and make you clean today.

Lord, I pray that You would touch me
with Your love, heal me with Your power,
and make me wholly clean. Amen.

The Promise of the Resurrection

"I am the resurrection and the life. He who believes
in Me, though he may die, he shall live."

JOHN 11:25 NKJV

Martin Luther said that "Our Lord has written the promise of the resurrection, not in books alone but in every leaf in spring-time." Each spring we watch the world wake up from the grave of winter. Life is resurrected in each leaf, each bloom, each blade of grass.

Springtime serves as a beautiful reminder of God's resurrection of Jesus from the grave—and of the promise His resurrection holds for us. Because the grave was not strong enough to hold Jesus, it will not hold us. One day we too will rise up from death and live with our Lord forever.

As you walk through the world this springtime, as you see God's creation shaking off the graveclothes of winter, as you see each leaf bursting forth into new life, be reminded of God's promise to give you new life. And praise Him for the riches of His grace.

*Lord, as I look around and see the wonders
of Your springtime, the new life where once
there was only cold death, I praise You for
the new life You have given me. Amen.*

Sing Anyway

Oh, sing to the LORD a new song!
Sing to the LORD, all the earth.
Sing to the LORD, bless His name;
Proclaim the good news of His salvation from day to day.

PSALM 96:1–2 NKJV

Sing to the Lord!

It doesn't matter how wonderful your voice is (or isn't), if you can hit the high C with ease or if you can't carry a note in that proverbial bucket. Sing anyway.

Whether the day has been filled with so many joys and blessings that you can't keep count or you've been knocked down so many times you can barely find the strength to crawl into bed at night, sing anyway.

It doesn't matter if everything is rosy or dark, if your heart is filled with joy or grief, or if you feel like singing or not . . . sing anyway.

Sing an old hymn, a new praise, your own song, or the wordless melody of your heart. Just sing to the God who created you, who loves you, and who showers you and saves you with His grace.

Lord, You are great, You are mighty, You are
my salvation. Hear me sing to You. Listen as
I pour out my heart in song. . . . Amen.

Changed

Later, Jesus showed himself to two of his followers
while they were walking in the country, but
he did not look the same as before.

MARK 16:12 NCV

After the Resurrection, Jesus did not look the same as He did before. After the arrest and the beatings, after the cross, and after the tomb, something was different.

When He died for our sins, Jesus was changed. And when you die *to* your sins, you also should be changed, inside and out. As your inner heart and soul are washed free of the burden and guilt of our sins, so your outer appearance should reflect the peace you have been given. Your actions should echo His grace as you reach out to the world around you to show them the love of your Savior.

Because grace should change the way you "look"—and it should change the way you look at others.

Lord, change me. Each day, make me—who I am
and the things I do and say—more like You. Amen.

God Knows You

*You have looked deep
into my heart, Lord, and you know all about me.*

PSALM 139:1 CEV

G od is unimaginably great and powerful, but He is also more personal than we could ever hope.

God *knows* you. He has looked into your heart and found every secret, every fear, every wonderful and dreadful and singular bit about you. He notices everything you do and everywhere you go (Psalm 139:3). He knows your every thought and your every word—even before you speak them (Psalm 139:4). He is the One Who knit you together, before you were born. He was the One Who created you, wonderfully and marvelously and thoughtfully (Psalm 139:13–14).

God knows everything you've ever said, or done, or tried to hide. And while that might seem frightening, it's actually freeing. Because God knows all there is to know, and He still loves you enough to send His Son to die for you. He still says to you: *Follow Me.*

Lord, You know everything there is to know about me. Even the things I'm afraid to tell anyone else. Yet You still love me and invite me to be part of Your kingdom. Thank You, Lord. Thank You. Amen.

Nowhere Without God

Where could I go to escape
from your Spirit
or from your sight?
PSALM 139:7 CEV

There is nowhere you can go that God is not with you. There is nowhere you can hide from Him or escape Him.

There is nowhere God can't find you. No sin is too big to keep you from Him. No distance is so far that He can't follow you there. No gulf is too wide for Him to bridge. If you climbed to the top of Mount Everest or sank to the depths of the Marianas Trench, if you jetted off to the other side of the Milky Way or beyond, God would see you. And not only that, but He would already be there in that moment and place, waiting for you to arrive. God is ready to guide and guard you, wherever you may go.

Lord, You are with me every step every
moment, ready to guide and to guard. Thank
You, Lord, for watching over me. Amen.

Size Them Up

"Look beneath the surface so you can judge correctly."
JOHN 7:24 NLT

What's the first thing you notice about people? Is it their clothes? Their hair or eyes? The way they talk or walk? The job they have or the kind of car they drive? Do you size them up and wonder, *I wonder what they can they do for me . . . ?*

Today, try to see others the way God sees them. Look beyond the clothes, the walk, or the talk. Instead, look at their heart. Open your eyes and see that insecure boy hiding inside the adult with his designer labels. See the worried girl behind the big desk wondering if she's really got what it takes. Look past the swaggering walk and the bragging talk to see the person hungry for approval, for love, for God. Size them up and wonder, *What can I do for them?*

Lord, help me to look at each person I meet today and see them as You see them, love them as You love them, and reach out to them as You would have me do. Amen.

Without Ceasing

Pray without ceasing.
1 THESSALONIANS 5:17 NKJV

"Pray without ceasing." Other translations say, "Never stop praying." And maybe you wonder, *How could anyone possibly pray without ceasing?* Because you have work to do, a family to tend, houses to clean, food to prepare . . . You really want to follow God in all things, but how could you possibly have time to pray constantly?

Perhaps it's time to reconsider your definition of "prayer." It's not always heads bowed, eyes closed, stillness before God. More often, it's an up-and-moving, ongoing conversation with God as you go through the busyness of your day. It's turning your heart toward Him like a sunflower turning toward the sun.

So let your thoughts naturally turn to Him to ask His opinions on the decisions of your day—even the little things. And keep your ear tuned to hear Him as He talks to you through His Spirit, through His Word, and through the people He sends into your life.

Prayer is a part of God's amazing gift of grace. So pray without ceasing, because God listens without ceasing.

*Lord, teach me to pray without ceasing so that
my prayers do not end when I say "Amen."*

Calm in the Chaos

I must calm down and turn to God;
only he can rescue me . . .
[H]e is my only hope.

PSALM 62:1, 5 ERV

This world can be anything but calm. Text alerts, email alerts, emergency alerts. Rush-hour traffic, ever-changing deadlines, ever-changing needs. The demands on your time, your energy, and your faith are relentless. Your stress level ratchets up, your heart pounds, and your head begins to throb. How could you possibly be calm in a time like this?

This isn't just a modern-day problem. It's a problem David struggled with too. Remind yourself, as he did, of the one perfect answer to the wildness of this world: *Calm down and turn to God.* Turn to God for hope, for rescue, for peace, and for calm in the midst of the chaos. Bringing peace to your storm is God's gift to you. So today, take a deep breath, calm down, and turn to God.

*Lord, when everything seems to be spinning around
and out of control, remind me to turn to You, to
allow You to breathe calm into the chaos. Amen.*

Pour Out

Trust in him at all times, you people;
pour out your hearts to him,
for God is our refuge.

PSALM 62:8 NIV

God is always ready to listen, no matter how small the concern or how huge the problem. He's there if you need to talk for a moment or for an hour. If you need to share anger, or sadness, or joy, or any other feeling, God is always there to listen. Not out of obligation. Not just because He said He would. But because He truly cares.

So pour out your heart to God. Empty it of all your troubles, heartaches, and disappointments, big and small. Pour out all your worries, fears, secrets, and shames. When you do, God pours in His mercy, His love, His peace, His strength, and His grace.

Lord, I pour out my heart to You now,
and I wait in Your presence for You to
pour Your grace into me. Amen.

He Will Be Found

"You will seek Me and find Me, when you
search for Me with all your heart."

JEREMIAH 29:13 NKJV

We tend to lose things, don't we? Some things we can find again, like lost keys or receipts or even friends. Other things can never be found again, like lost time or opportunities.

But sometimes we lose God—or perhaps it's just that we lose sight of Him because we've turned away from Him and turned to the world instead. And when we realize the magnitude of that loss, we search *desperately*.

This is when we can lay claim to His beautiful promise: When we search for Him with all our hearts, He will be found. And when we find Him, we discover that He's been right there all along, chasing after us, because "doesn't [a shepherd] leave the ninety-nine [sheep] in the open country and go after the lost sheep until he finds it?" (Luke 15:4 NIV).

Do you need to search for God today? You'll soon discover that He's been with you the whole time.

*Lord, I'm so grateful that You do not hide
Yourself from me. Thank You for being a
God who wants to be found. Amen.*

MAY

The Comfort of the Ordinary

Jesus held her hand and called to her, "Little girl, stand up!" Her spirit came back into her, and she stood up immediately. Jesus said, "Give her something to eat."

LUKE 8:54–55 ERV

Jairus's daughter was dead. The sounds of weeping filled the air. Then Jesus came, took her hand, and said, "Stand up!" And she did! What's the very next thing that Jesus said? "Behold"? "Call the presses"? "Go forth and live a brilliant life"?

No. Jesus said, "Give her something to eat." It seems a bit . . . well, *ordinary*, doesn't it?

Maybe this is because Jesus understands the power of ordinary things to bring comfort. This family had had a jarring day—from the despair of death to the miracle of life restored. The simple acts of preparing and eating a meal would bring a blessed bit of the ordinary back into their suddenly extraordinary lives.

When you have a jarring day, pull yourself back with a blessed bit of the ordinary. Eat, work, sleep. Pray, read, trust. Let the power of the ordinary comfort you, because this is where we can find God too.

Lord, I thank You for the blessings of the ordinary. Let me find comfort in the simple routines of my day today. Amen.

Right There with You

He said to his followers, "Where is your faith?"
LUKE 8:25 ERV

In Luke 8, we find the disciples out in their boat. As the storm blows in, their courage blows out. In their fear and fright, the disciples do exactly the right thing: They run to Jesus, who is sleeping at one end of the boat. "Teacher, don't you care about us?" they ask. "We are going to drown!" (Mark 4:38 ERV). Jesus stands, and at His words, the wind stills, the waves stop, and the disciples stand amazed. But Jesus has a question for them: "Where is your faith?" Because He was right there with them in the boat: He would never have let anything happen to them.

When you're stuck in a storm—of rain, of trouble, of busyness—where is your faith? Do you run to Jesus and ask if He cares? Your Savior is right there with you in the boat.

Lord, strengthen my faith in You. Help me to see this day that You are always right there with me. Amen.

Trusting God

*Oh, the depth of the riches both of the wisdom
and knowledge of God! How unsearchable are His
judgments and His ways past finding out!*

<small>ROMANS 11:33 NKJV</small>

The way God thinks—the way He works in our lives and in this world—is impossible for us to understand. But He is the One—*the only One*—who has never and will never let us down.

And so we trust Him. We follow Him down the path He lays before us. No, we don't know where it leads. And, yes, that is more than a little frightening sometimes. But He is with us, side by side, step by step. He will guide us in the way we should go. He will shield and protect and shelter us.

As we hold fast to His hand, He promises to never let go of ours. And by His grace, we travel this path, *His path*, together with Him . . . today and always.

*Holy Father, I don't always understand the
direction You are leading me, but I trust You and
I will follow You all the days of my life. Amen.*

Joy in the Storm

When troubles of any kind come your way,
consider it an opportunity for great joy.

JAMES 1:2 NLT

Have you ever watched a storm roll in? When you're safely settled in a front porch swing, or inside looking out, watching a storm roll in can be fascinating and beautiful. The wind whips the trees and sends leaves and random bits of paper skittering along. Rain hurtles down, lightning zings across the sky, and the thunder rumbles across the sky. But you? You are safely settled under the shelter, just watching the storm roll in, with nothing to fear. You have joy.

But what about when the storm rolling in isn't found in the sky? When the rumbles aren't thunder or lightning but skirmishes with enemies? Where is the joy in those storms? It's not in the wind or the rains; it's in the sheltering arms of Jesus. *He* will be your joy in the storm.

Lord Jesus, You shelter me through the storms,
not only keeping me safe, but giving me joy.
Thank You, Jesus, thank You! Amen.

Love and Grace

God is love.

1 JOHN 4:8 NIV

God *is love.*

God isn't the imperfect, sometimes selfish, often changeable love we offer each other. God's love for each of us is perfect: It is without end, without conditions, and without limits.

It was God's perfect love that sent Jesus to earth, to the cross, to the grave, and to life again. His perfect love forgives, restores, and redeems. And His perfect love declares that "nothing can separate us from God's love—not life or death, not angels or spirits, not the present or the future, and not powers above or powers below. Nothing in all creation can separate us from God's love for us in Christ Jesus our Lord!" (Romans 8:38–39 CEV).

It is God's perfect love that gives us His perfect grace.

*Your love is unending, Your grace is unfathomable,
and together they are unbelievably powerful and
unimaginably wonderful to me. Thank You,
Lord, for Your perfect love and grace. Amen.*

Only One Thing

"Martha, Martha! You are worried and upset about so many things, but only one thing is necessary. Mary has chosen what is best, and it will not be taken away from her."

LUKE 10:41–42 CEV

Jesus was staying at the home of Mary and Martha. And while Martha hurried about "doing all the work that had to be done" (Luke 10:40 ERV), Mary sat at the feet of Jesus and listened to Him teach. You probably know how the rest goes. When Martha complained that Mary wasn't helping, Jesus gently pointed out that only one thing was truly necessary: Him.

Sometimes it's a question of right or wrong, good versus evil. But more often it's a question of good versus best. Sometimes you have to give yourself permission to let the email and the dishes wait. Don't worry if you can write your name in the dust on the mantel. You can leave some things till later. But always make time for Jesus—to sit quietly at His feet and listen as He speaks to you.

Lord Jesus, please give me the wisdom to choose between good and best—the willpower to do it. Amen.

But for the Grace of God

"Don't judge others, and God will not judge you."
Matthew 7:1 erv

"**D**on't judge." It's a phrase our culture likes to toss around—a bit like a weapon—to silence anyone who would distinguish between right and wrong. But society tends to only look at the words that fit its own agenda. Notice what the next verse says: "If you judge others, you will be judged the same way you judge them. God will treat you the same way you treat others" (Matthew 7:2 erv).

It's not that you should never declare something is wrong; rather, it's injecting grace—the same grace you hope God gives you—into your judgments. It's not focusing on the speck in your neighbor's eyes while having a plank in your own (Matthew 7:3–5). Always remember: There but for the grace of God go *you*.

Lord, please forgive me for judging others unfairly. Help me to focus on getting rid of the sin in my own life rather than pointing out the sins of others. Amen.

With God

When the angel of the Lord appeared to Gideon,
he said, "The Lord is with you, mighty warrior."

JUDGES 6:12 NIV

G ideon was from the weakest clan in the tribe, and he was the weakest in his own family. So he wasn't exactly the poster boy for a mighty warrior. In fact, when the angel of the Lord appeared to him and called him "mighty," Gideon was cowering in the bottom of a winepress, threshing out wheat and hoping to hide the grain from his enemies. How could the Lord have seen him as a mighty warrior?

The answer lies in the few words right before "mighty warrior": "The Lord is with you." Or, as another translation says, "The Lord is helping you" (CEV). Because whoever you are, wherever or whatever you're hiding, you too can be a mighty warrior for the Lord . . . with His help.

As you face the world today, remember that you are a "mighty warrior" because God is fighting at your side.

Holy Father, instead of focusing on all the things
I can't do or am afraid to do, help me see all
that I can do with You helping me. Amen.

Small Blessings

But Jesus said, "Let the children come to me." . . . And he placed his hands on their heads and blessed them before he left.

MATTHEW 19:14–15 NLT

Jesus did some pretty miraculous and amazing things in His ministry on earth—like walking on water, stilling storms, and raising the dead to life. But He also did some small and beautiful things—like hugging children, weeping with a friend, and having a talk with a woman by a well.

These things may have seemed small to the world, but they were monumental to those children, that friend, and that woman by the well. And they were pretty big things to God. After all, He included them in His Book, where they're still changing thoughts and lives today.

Is it a blessing to be able to do big things for God, things all the world can see? Absolutely! But it is no less a blessing to do the small things no one but God sees. You might not change the world, but you could change someone's world—and their eternity.

What little things can you do today?

Lord, show me how I can serve You. What "small" things can I do for You today? Amen.

A Greater Love

As a mother comforts her child,
so will I comfort you . . .
ISAIAH 66:13 NIV

D o you remember being held in your mother's arms? Do you remember the unquestioning comfort you found in them as a child? There should be no safer place in this world than being wrapped in your mother's arms, nowhere you feel more loved.

Maybe you didn't have that kind of mom. Maybe her arms weren't a place of comfort and safety. Maybe she didn't show you her love. But an even greater kind of love and comfort and safety can be yours—in the arms of God. He will heal your heart when it's broken (Psalm 147:3), soothe away your fears (Isaiah 41:10), and comfort you in the midst of your sorrows (2 Corinthians 1:3–4). Because His love is greater—infinitely greater—than any mother's love.

Lord, wrap me in Your unending love.
Shelter and comfort me. Let me hide in
You, just for a little while. Amen.

The Heart of God

"My thoughts are nothing like your thoughts," says the LORD.
"And my ways are far beyond anything you could imagine.
For just as the heavens are higher than the earth,
so my ways are higher than your ways
and my thoughts higher than your thoughts."
ISAIAH 55:8–9 NLT

When God looks at you, He "does not look at the things people look at. People look at the outward appearance, but the LORD looks at the heart" (1 Samuel 16:7 NIV).

Do you do the same for Him?

When you don't understand what God is doing or why; when you don't understand how He could allow something to happen or not happen; when you don't understand the path He has asked you to follow, or why He has asked you to abandon the one you were on—do you try to look into His heart?

It is impossible for us to understand God's ways. This side of heaven, we'll never comprehend why He does what He does or thinks the things that He thinks. But we can know the heart behind them . . . His heart, which is always good (Nahum 1:7 NIV).

Lord, there are so many times I don't understand
what You are doing in my life or why. But
please help me remember that You are
always working for my good. Amen.

A Home with God

Even the sparrow finds a home,
and the swallow builds her nest and raises her young
at a place near your altar,
O Lord of Heaven's Armies, my King and my God!
PSALM 84:3 NLT

A home with God. Is there any thought more lovely, more comforting, or more sustaining? One day we will be free of this life's troubles, sorrows, and sins. As beloved children of God, we will find our permanent home with our Lord in the New Jerusalem.

But we don't have to wait for the afterlife to find a home with God. Even the sparrow and the swallow have found a place to nest near His altar. And Matthew 10:29–31 tells us that they are ever under His watchful care, for "not one of them will fall to the ground outside your Father's care. And even the very hairs of your head are all numbered. So don't be afraid; you are worth more than many sparrows" (NIV).

You don't have to wait for heaven in order to live with God. You can dwell in His presence right now, today (Psalm 84:1)—singing His praises your whole life.

Lord, teach me to make my home with you.
I'd rather be a doorkeeper with You than
rule the earth without You. Amen.

Love Yourself

"Love others as much as you love yourself."

MARK 12:31 CEV

*L*ove *others as much as you love yourself.* We spend a lot of time on the first part of this commandment from Jesus, but almost none on the second part. Yes, you must love others, but how should you love them? *As much as you love yourself.* Which means you must also love yourself.

Did you cringe a bit at that? So often, we see loving yourself as vain, self-indulgent, even sinful—and it can be if we ignore the "love others" part of the commandment too. But consider this: God Himself loves you endlessly, and He is unfailingly kind to you. So why would you ever be anything less than kind and loving to yourself?

Today, take time to care for yourself. Use kind words and be gentle with yourself. Love yourself.

*Lord, help me see and understand that loving myself
is not a sinful thing but rather a part of loving You—
because You are the One Who made me. Amen.*

The Shadow of God

Give yourselves completely to God. Stand against
the devil, and the devil will run from you.

JAMES 4:7 NCV

I t's so easy for us to simply take the second part of this verse and run with it: "Stand against the devil . . ." Some translations say to "resist" the devil. When we do, he will run from you. These words alone make it sound like we hold this power over him in our own right.

But the real power of this promise isn't in us. It's in those words we too often skip over: "Give yourselves completely to God." Standing up to the devil on your own is a recipe for disaster. But when you surrender the control of your life to God, you become His child. You instantly inherit all the rights of being His child—including having your Father stand up and fight for you.

So when the devil sets you in his sights, he can't help but see the shadow of the Almighty God standing behind you. And *that's* what sends him running.

Lord, help me never forget that the best way to stand
against the devil is to bow down to You. Amen.

Enough

"There's a young boy here with five barley loaves and two fish. But what good is that with this huge crowd?"

JOHN 6:9 NLT

The disciples stared out at the hungry crowd. There were thousands and thousands of them—men, women, and even children! Where would they find enough food to feed all those people? And even if they found enough food, how would they ever pay for it? Sure, one boy had given up his lunch. (Don't you just love that little guy's selflessness?) But what good were five loaves and two fish when they needed to feed thousands? Still, Jesus took the little boy's lunch, thanked God for it, and . . . it was enough.

Maybe you're looking at what you have to offer God's kingdom and thinking, *What good is this? How can something so little even make a dent?* Trust, believe, and do what Jesus did. Offer what you have today to God, thank Him for it, and He will make it enough. Because it's not what you have that matters; it's who you give it to.

Lord, I feel like what I have to offer isn't even enough to matter. But I understand that what truly matters is giving it to You. So I give You this day all that I have. Amen.

Interrupted

When Jesus landed and saw a large crowd, he had
compassion on them, because they were like sheep without
a shepherd. So he began teaching them many things.

MARK 6:34 NIV

J esus had other plans that day. He and His disciples were actually trying to escape the crowds to get just a little time to rest. But the crowds followed them. And when Jesus saw them, His heart ached when He saw how lost they were. *He had compassion on them.* Yes, the people interrupted Jesus's plans. They often did. But did He respond with anger or irritation? No. He responded with love, and He gave them that which they needed most: a way back to God.

The next time your plans are interrupted, stop and consider for a moment: Is this really just another aggravating interruption? Or is it an opportunity to help someone see God? It's certainly okay to postpone or even say no to those unnecessary interruptions that clog up your day. Just take a moment to make sure you aren't saying no to God.

Lord, teach me to see the difference between
ordinary interruptions and opportunities to
serve You. Help me never to miss a chance
to help someone else find You. Amen.

An Undivided Heart

Teach me your way, LORD,
that I may rely on your faithfulness;
give me an undivided heart,
that I may fear your name.

PSALM 86:11 NIV

David's prayer from so long ago is timeless; it could—and should—be our prayer today. God's way is perfect, abounding in mercy, goodness, and love for everyone who calls on His name (Psalm 86:5). We can always rely on God, because—unlike the ever-changing "truths" of this world—His truth never changes.

By following God's way, we nurture an *undivided heart* within ourselves, which is so precious to God. An undivided heart is one that knows that God alone is Lord of all. Its loyalties are not divided between God and the here-today-and-done-tomorrow treasures of this world. Such a heart loves the Lord with all its heart, soul, mind, and strength.

Is your heart an undivided heart? How can you begin to rely on God's faithfulness today?

Lord, I pray—as David did—that You would teach me Your ways and create in me an undivided heart that loves You above all else. Amen.

Stepping on Toes

If we say we love God and don't love each other, we are liars. We cannot see God. So how can we love God, if we don't love the people we can see?

1 JOHN 4:20 CEV

Ouch! Did these words from 1 John step on your spiritual toes? Admit it: There are those people you just really don't care for, aren't there? Of course, you can rationalize your lack of love: *God, she betrayed me. He left me. They refused my friendship and laughed at me. She stole. He lied. They're unkind. They don't love You.*

But do you think any of those reasons means anything to God? This is the same God who told us to love our enemies (Matthew 5:44) and then sent His own Son to prove that He did. The question you have to answer is in the second half of the verse: If you can't love the people you can see, how can you love God—the One you can't see?

God's Word has a way of stepping on your toes when He wants to get your attention. Is He stepping on your toes today? What will you do about it?

Lord, I have plenty of excuses for why I don't love some people. But my excuses don't excuse me from Your command. Help me to truly love You by truly loving them. Amen.

Anyway

> "Seek first his kingdom and his righteousness, and
> all these things will be given to you as well."
>
> MATTHEW 6:33 NIV

You're so busy. Surely it wouldn't hurt to skip your prayers for just one day? You're so tired. What could it hurt to watch a movie instead of reading your Bible? You haven't had a chance to relax in so long. It will probably be okay to miss church just this one day.

You're so tired, so busy, so frazzled, so . . . *seek God anyway*. Talk to God and tell Him you're tired. He may not give you sleep, but He'll give your restless spirit a peace too great to understand. Read His Word. Let Him show you what is truly important in this life—and what you could simply let go of. And gather with others who love Him. As you lift up your voices to praise Him together, God will renew and restore you. Today, show God you love Him.

*Lord, it's so easy for me to make an excuse to
neglect You. I'm sorry. Please remind me that
all those things I crave—rest and stillness and
renewal—are the things I find in You. Amen.*

The Next Step

I will instruct you and teach you in the way
you should go; I will guide you . . .

PSALM 32:8 NKJV

How do you like to travel? Are you a carefree, fly-by-the-seat-of-your-pants kind of person who just hits the road without even a definite destination in mind? Or are you a plan-it-all-out, even-scheduling-the-potty-stops kind of person?

When your journey is just for fun, you can do it your own way. But when heaven is your destination, God's way is the only way to get there. Don't worry, though. He'll teach you how to go and guide you along the way.

But you'll have to trust Him. Because even though God knows every last detail of the trip, He won't share them all with you. Instead, He'll show you the next step, the next turn, the next little bit of the road. And when you reach that, He'll show the next one . . . all the way home.

Lord, please show me the next step to
take toward heaven today. Amen.

So Completely

He takes care of me completely!

PSALM 57:2 ERV

Have you ever stopped to consider all the different ways God takes care of you?

Each morning He greets you with a fresh sunrise. He fills your day with the whisper of the wind, the ever-changing blue of the skies, and the faces of other people. And each evening He tucks you in by the light of the moon.

His Word speaks to your heart and heals your spirit. His presence shields and protects you. His love covers and fills you. From the oxygen you breathe to the food you eat, from the ones who love you to the Savior who saves you, heart and mind, body and soul—God takes care of you.

Slow down today. Notice all the different ways God provides for you. And then thank Him for taking care of you so completely.

Holy Father God, there is so much You do that I take for granted. Thank You for taking care of me so completely. Amen.

It's Okay to Say No

This is what I want:
Let me live in the LORD's house
all my life.
Let me see the LORD's beauty
and look with my own eyes at his Temple.

PSALM 27:4 NCV

S ome people will tell you it isn't okay to say no. And, let's be honest, they're usually the people who want you to say yes to something. But it's your choice. And you can choose to say no.

You can say no to bad things, of course. But you can also say no to good things and, yes, even to church things: that extra project, that be-the-team-parent role, that bring-the-casserole thing, and that teach-the-class thing. Sometimes you need to turn down those things so that you can say yes to God—even if that yes is simply sitting quietly at the feet of your Lord, talking to Him, and listening as He speaks to your heart.

Do you need to say no to someone or something today so that you can say yes to God?

Lord, it sometimes seems as if there is a steady stream of people wanting me to do something. Help me to choose my yeses wisely and to know when I should say no. Amen.

Yesterday Is Not Today

Good people might fall again and
again, but they always get up.

PROVERBS 24:16 ERV

Yesterday . . . well, maybe yesterday you blew it. You did what you said you wouldn't. You yelled when you knew you shouldn't. And you failed when you thought you couldn't.

So you ended the day on your knees, begging for forgiveness and knowing you had let Him down yet again. But that was yesterday. Today is today. And today is a new day.

It's time to get up, to dust yourself off, and to try again. Today you've been given a whole new chance to *not* repeat yesterday's mistakes. Leave the regrets of yesterday in the past. Love and serve your God today.

*Lord, I don't want to waste time worrying
over yesterday's mistakes. Rather, help
me live for You today. Amen.*

When You'd Rather Not

Remember that the Lord will give you
an inheritance as your reward, and that
the Master you are serving is Christ.

COLOSSIANS 3:24 NLT

There are parts of serving Jesus that are a delight. These things are usually different for each person. For some it's singing praises to God, for others it's rocking babies in the nursery, and for still others it's cooking a comforting meal for someone who's hurting. Then there are those parts of serving that we'd really rather not do.

When you have to serve in a way you'd rather not, remember the reward God has waiting for you: your inheritance in heaven. Let thoughts of that reward carry you through and help you do what you need to do. God sees, and by His grace He will reward you—not so much because of the things you do, but because you do them for Him.

*Lord, it's true, there are some parts of serving
that I would rather leave for others to do.
Forgive me, and help me remember that You
are the reason I do the things I do. Amen.*

Daily

Praise be to the Lord, to God our Savior,
who daily bears our burdens.

PSALM 68:19 NIV

God bears your burdens every day. The burdens that change all the time, that ebb and flow with the times and the seasons of your life. The big and the small. The dramas and the dangers. The cancer and the cold. God will bear them all for you . . . *if* you lay them in His hands and entrust them to Him.

You know in your head that your worrying can't do a single bit of good, but your heart still struggles to let your burdens go. God understands that struggle. He really does. But He also knows relief can only come from Him. So He stretches out His hand and softly whispers, *Give them to Me. Let Me carry your load today.*

Lord, these burdens I carry are too heavy for me.
Take them. I entrust them to You—to fix them,
finish them, or just see me through them. Amen.

Be Still

"Be still, and know that I am God . . ."
PSALM 46:10 NIV

*B*e still. It means to sink down, relax, and let go. Other Bible translations say, "Calm down" (CEV), "Stop fighting" (ERV), and "Cease *striving*" (NASB).

Sink down, relax, let go. Calm down, stop, cease, and know that:

God is Lord of All Creation, and He created you.

God is in control, so He can take care of you.

God is alive, and death is no match for Him.

God is with you and will never, not for an instant, leave your side.

God is love, and He loves you.

Stop right now. Be still. And get to know God.

Lord, I sit here quietly with You in breathless anticipation. Show me who You are. . . . I want to know You. Amen.

Have You?

"Return to your own house, and tell what great things God has done for you." And he went his way and proclaimed throughout the whole city what great things Jesus had done for him.

LUKE 8:39 NKJV

Jesus cast a legion of demons out of the man in the verse above. Imagine how grateful he must have been. He wanted to go with Jesus, to follow the One Who had given him back his life. Wouldn't you? But Jesus sent him home with this one command: "Tell what great things God has done for you." And that's exactly what the man did.

Have you?

Jesus may not have cast a legion of demons out of you, but He has certainly saved you from an eternity spent with the likes of them. So, have you done what that man did? Have you told everyone about the great things God has done for you? Today, take a moment to consider all the Lord has done for you, then go and tell someone about it.

Lord, show me someone today who needs to hear about You. And then please give me the words and the courage to tell of the great things You have done for me. Amen.

Your Name

"He calls his own sheep by name and leads them out."

JOHN 10:3 NIV

Jesus calls your name because He is the Good Shepherd, and He knows His sheep *personally*.

Jesus knows everything you've done—every secret, every sin, every shame you've tried to hide. And He knows everything you haven't done: every time you haven't given or helped; every time you've walked away when you should have stayed; every time you've denied Him.

Still . . . Jesus calls your name. Because He knows how much you need His love and how desperately you need His grace. His compassions are there for you, fresh and new every morning, no matter yesterday's mistakes (Lamentations 3:22–23). Jesus is calling your name even now. All you have to do is answer Him.

Lord Jesus, I am overwhelmed by the fact that the Lord of All Creation calls my name! I am answering, "Lord, I am Yours!" Amen.

Knocking

"Look! I stand at the door and knock. If you hear
my voice and open the door, I will come in, and
we will share a meal together as friends."

REVELATION 3:20 NLT

R evelation 3:20 holds some of the Bible's most beautiful promises. You are blessed with a Savior Who is not content simply to sit in heaven, hoping you'll one day seek Him out. No, your Savior comes to you and knocks on the door of your heart. He won't force Himself in: The choice to open the door or leave it closed is always yours. But He will continue to knock until you open or until death seals the door forever.

Oh, but if you hear His knock and you open that door, Jesus steps in—into your heart, into your life, into your eternity—as your Friend. If you haven't opened that door and claimed Jesus as your Friend, don't wait any longer. Open the door today.

Lord Jesus, who am I that You would come
to me, to knock on the door of my heart?
But I am so thankful that You do, and I
open my heart's door to You. Amen.

David's Prayer

You, Lord, are forgiving and good,
abounding in love to all who call to you. . . .
[Y]ou, Lord, are a compassionate and gracious God,
slow to anger, abounding in love and faithfulness.
PSALM 86:5, 15 NIV

Psalm 86 is actually a prayer. The psalmist—many believe it was David—wrote this prayer while under attack by vicious enemies. But he doesn't blame God for his troubles. In fact, notice the words and phrases he uses to describe God: "forgiving," "good," "compassionate," "gracious," "slow to anger," "abounding in love and faithfulness." In spite of his enemies' attacks—or perhaps because of them—David praises God simply for who He is.

Do we do the same? When we're under attack—whether it's from enemies or illness or just a really rough day—do we praise God simply for who He is? Or do we turn away from Him or even shake our fists at Him in anger for not shielding us from trouble? The next time you're feeling under attack, remember David and his prayer. Praise God simply for Who He is. Because He is so loving and gracious and good, He cannot help but answer you (Psalm 86:7).

Holy Father, even when troubles come my
way, I know that You are so good—and so
good to me. I love You, Lord. Amen.

Default Settings

For you created my inmost being;
you knit me together in my mother's womb.

PSALM 139:13 NIV

Whether it's a phone, computer, or smart TV, it seems almost everything electronic has a default setting. It's the way the creator originally intended the product to be. But we like to tinker a little here and there, personalize things, adding to and taking away to make them work better for us. And sometimes they do, but sometimes things can get completely messed up and need to be restored to the default settings.

We're not much different. God created each of us with default settings—the way He intended for us to be. But we like to tinker here and there, to personalize our approach to God and life. And sometimes we can really mess things up. That's when we need to be restored to our default settings: "Be kind and compassionate to one another, forgiving each other, just as in Christ God forgave you" (Ephesians 4:32 NIV).

Do you need to be restored today?

Lord, help me to take a good look at myself today. Show me those areas in my life that need to be restored to Your default settings. Amen.

JUNE

Grace Is Love

The Spirit produces the fruit of love . . .

GALATIANS 5:22 NCV

When the Holy Spirit of God comes to live inside you, He isn't just present in your life. The Spirit is *busy* in your life. And the more you turn the ear of your heart to Him and listen as He leads you, the more He will teach you how to be like God.

Because "God is love" (1 John 4:8 NIV), as you listen to the Spirit and follow Him, you will learn how to reflect God's love into the world around you. His love is not like the love of the world, which says love means accepting all things. Rather, God's love is one that cares enough to gently correct and lovingly lead others to Him. It doesn't love differently based on age or race or gender. It doesn't care about bank accounts or titles. It seeks the best for all people, simply because we all share the same Father and God.

God's grace reveals itself in love.

*Holy Father, teach me to listen to Your Spirit
working inside me. Teach me to love like You—
without conditions and without limits. Amen.*

Grace Is Joy

The Spirit produces the fruit of . . . joy . . .
GALATIANS 5:22 NCV

Joy is more than being happy.

Happiness comes from ourselves, from the things and people of this world. When the skies are blue and everything is going our way, happiness is laughter in the sunshine.

Joy comes from the Holy Spirit. It may be accompanied by the happiness found in the people and things of this world, or it may not. Joy happens whether the skies are blue . . . or when they are storm filled. We experience joy when everything is going our way . . . and when everything seems stacked against us. Joy is laughter in the sunshine . . . and sweet, holy comfort in the rain.

Joy is knowing that no matter what this day—this life— holds, God is always with you, and He has a plan, a purpose, and a home in heaven waiting for you.

Because God's grace reveals itself in joy.

Lord, thank You for Your presence and Your promises—including the promise of Your unending joy. Amen.

Grace Is Peace

The Spirit produces the fruit of . . . peace . . .
GALATIANS 5:22 NCV

When Jesus spoke to His disciples about returning to heaven, He gave them a promise: "I am leaving you with a gift—peace of mind and heart" (John 14:27 NLT). That peace is also for you, and you can claim it when you choose to follow Jesus. His peace comes through the Holy Spirit living and working within you.

The peace of God is unlike any sort of peace the world has to offer. Worldly peace comes and goes. It doesn't last because it depends on everything going just as it "should." But God's peace is greater: It's yours to have, to hold, to keep—even when nothing goes as it "should." Worldly peace is about control and being confident in your own abilities to take care of yourself, no matter what comes. John 14:27 tells us that heavenly peace allows you to face even the greatest of troubles without fear. You know the One Who is ultimately in control, and you trust Him to take care of you.

God's grace reveals itself in peace.

Lord, I trust You to take care of me. Even when I don't understand what is happening or why or how it will work out, I trust You—and that gives me peace. Amen.

Grace Is Patience

The Spirit produces the fruit of . . . patience . . .
GALATIANS 5:22 NCV

We don't see a lot of patience in our culture. How many times have you found yourself tapping your foot while waiting on the microwave to warm your coffee, or been in such a hurry that you had to stop and wait for the automatic door to *finally* open?

Patience is a struggle for us, but it is a crucial part of Who God is—and we should be so grateful! Because "the Lord . . . is being patient for your sake. He does not want anyone to be destroyed, but wants everyone to repent" (2 Peter 3:9 NLT). As the Spirit works in you, then you too will learn to be more patient. Patient with others as you gently try to lead them to God. Patient with yourself as you learn to be patient. And even patient with God as you wait for Him to unveil His perfect plan in His own perfect time.

Because God is endlessly patient with you, His grace reveals itself in patience.

Lord, thank You for being so patient with me. Let me offer that same patience to those around me—and to myself. Amen.

Grace Is Kindness

The Spirit produces the fruit of . . . kindness . . .

GALATIANS 5:22 NCV

It's the little things. The things you don't have to do. The things that perhaps no one ever sees.

It's giving when you don't have to. It's doing what you could have left for others to do. It's being there when no one else chooses to be.

What is it? It's *kindness*. And it stems from the Holy Spirit working inside you. Kindness doesn't seek attention, and it's not trying to put on a show. Rather, it seeks to give back a little of what has been given—that ultimate kindness of the cross.

Go out today and be kind, quietly kind. God will see your kindness and reward it with His own.

Because grace reveals itself in kindness.

Holy Father, You have been so kind to me and in so many ways. Show me how I can share some of that kindness with those around me today. Amen.

Grace Is Goodness

The Spirit produces the fruit of . . . goodness . . .
GALATIANS 5:22 NCV

When the Spirit works in you, goodness becomes a part of you. This kind of goodness isn't just about the things you do. It is a matter of actions, but it's also about the attitude of your heart.

Yes, "Jesus went everywhere doing good . . . because God was with him" (Acts 10:38 NCV). He helped and He healed. But the motive behind all the good things He did was not because there was some heavenly checklist of good deeds to be completed before He returned to heaven. Jesus did good everywhere He went for two reasons: first, because of His great love and compassion for the people (in other words, He *wanted* to do good); and second, to show people the goodness of God and lead them to Him.

Because God's grace reveals itself in goodness.

Lord, please use Your Spirit to create within me a genuine desire to reflect Your goodness into this world. Show me how I can do that today. Amen.

Grace Is Faithfulness

The Spirit produces the fruit of . . . faithfulness . . .

GALATIANS 5:22 NCV

Faithfulness is about keeping promises, about doing what you say you will do, about showing up when you say you will. It's being a person of integrity and honor. And it's something that God is perfect at. The Lord is unfailingly faithful, keeping every single one of His promises to us—including the one about covering our less-than-perfect faithfulness with His grace. Timothy reminds us that even "if we are faithless, he remains faithful, for he cannot disown himself" (2 Timothy 2:13 NIV).

As the Holy Spirit lives and works in you, He will teach you to be more faithful. He will teach you not only to keep your promises to others but also to keep your promises to God—to faithfully follow and obey Him.

God's grace reveals itself in faithfulness—and helps us be faithful in return.

Lord, please show me those places in my life where I have not been faithful to my promises—and lead me to be more faithful from this day on. Amen.

Grace Is Gentleness

The Spirit produces the fruit of . . . gentleness.
GALATIANS 5:23 NCV

Gentleness is not something you're likely to see in the latest Hollywood blockbuster; our world usually considers it a weakness. Perhaps you haven't given it much thought, either. But if you've ever been left reeling by the harshness of the world and then touched by someone's gentleness, you know how priceless it really is.

Because it's the gentle answer that "turns away wrath" (Proverbs 15:1 NIV) and the gentle correction that restores people to God (Galatians 6:1). Gentleness is a "whisper," the still, small voice of God that comforts and guides you (1 Kings 19:12 NIV). It's the Savior who offers to carry your burdens and teach you His ways (Matthew 11:28–29). Gentleness is always treating others with the same gift of grace that you've been given.

Because God's grace reveals itself in gentleness.

Holy Father, You have been so gentle with me. Teach my heart to be gentle with those whose paths I cross today. Amen.

Grace Is Self-Control

The Spirit produces the fruit of . . . self-control.
GALATIANS 5:23 NCV

Sometimes it takes superhuman strength to not lose your cool or blow your top. Sometimes it's a battle not to sink to your knees in sadness or cower in the corner in fear. And sometimes it's all you can do not to walk right into that sin—the very one you've resisted for so long.

When feelings threaten to overwhelm you, when sin seems determined to sink its teeth into you, superhuman strength is what you need—and it's superhuman strength that God gives you. The Holy Spirit living within you is there to guide, to teach, and to protect you. But He is also there to strengthen and empower you. Remember, the same power that raised up Jesus from the dead *lives* inside you (Romans 8:11–14)! When you are struggling, reach out to the Holy Spirit. He will help you.

Because God's grace reveals itself in self-control.

*Holy Father, so often it's hard to do what I
know is right. Strengthen me with Your Spirit
so that I will always follow You. Amen.*

The First Step

"So he returned home to his father."
LUKE 15:20 NLT

Have you heard the story of the "first step"? No? Well, perhaps you know it by one of its more familiar names: the story of the "lost son" or the "prodigal son."

You see, there was a young man who didn't want to wait for his inheritance, so he went to his father and demanded his share immediately. Clutching his coins, the son then went off into the big, wide, wild world, where he wasted his money away. Only when he was left with nothing did he realize that the greatest of his father's treasures wasn't land or coins; it was his love and care. The young man rose up from the slop he had sunk into and took that first step back toward his father and his home. A second step followed the first and then a third . . . until his father ran to welcome him home.

Have you wandered out into the big, wide, wild world only to discover that the greatest of treasures is your Father's love and care? It isn't lost to you. Just take that first step toward Him—and He'll come running to welcome you home.

Lord, forgive me for the times I lose sight of the greatest treasure of all: living in Your perfect love and care. Amen.

What Does the Father Do?

"He ran to his son, threw his arms around him and kissed him."

LUKE 15:20 NIV

What does the Father do when you wander away from Him and then come back again? Whether your leaving just sort of happened a little bit at a time or you shook your fist at Him and stormed away, what does God do when you return?

Is there a heaping helping of guilt and shame waiting for you? Is there a list of punishments to endure? Or will He simply turn away from you? No. Nope. Never.

God is the One Who sets you free from shame and guilt, for "there is now no condemnation for those who are in Christ Jesus" (Romans 8:1 NIV). There's no punishment waiting from Him: Jesus is "the atoning sacrifice for our sins" (1 John 2:2 NIV). And He never turns His back on you: "He will never leave you or forsake you" (Deuteronomy 31:8 NIV).

If you really want to know what the Father will do, just look at the father's reaction to the return of his lost son: "He ran to his son, threw his arms around him and kissed him."

*Holy Father, I can only wonder at the depth
of Your love, and I can only praise You for
the amazing gift of Your grace. Amen.*

Nothing to Offer

"Father, I have sinned against God and against you. I am no
longer worthy to be called your son, but let me be like one
of your servants." So the son left and went to his father.

LUKE 15:18–20 NCV

When the prodigal son returned home to his father, he
had nothing to offer. No money, no gifts, no reputa-
tion. All he had was sorrow for the life he'd thrown away and
the sinful things he'd done. As he came before his father, he
didn't dare claim his place in the family. He only begged for
shelter. But the father took one look at his humbled heart and
restored him as his son.

In much the same way, we have nothing to offer—not to
God. He doesn't care about our money, our gifts, our worldly
achievements, or our reputations. After all, "the cattle on a
thousand hills" belong to Him (Psalm 50:10 NIV). Our sins mean
we have no claim to His family name. Yet, when we bow before Him with humble and repenting hearts, in His infinite
grace He lifts us up and calls us His own.

*Holy Father, my sins are so many, and I have
nothing to offer You, except myself. And that I
give You—heart, mind, body, and soul. Amen.*

No Wonder

My heart is confident in you, O God;
my heart is confident.
No wonder I can sing your praises!

PSALM 57:7 NLT

You've seen what God has done, and you know what God can do. You've seen it in the Bible, and you've known His power in your own life. You've put your trust in Him, and He's always come through. So it's no wonder your soul wants to sing!

Pour your heart into songs of praise to the One Who loves you endlessly, cares for you completely, and saves you eternally with the gift of His grace. It doesn't matter if you can't carry a tune or if you miss every note. Your sweet songs of praise are precious to the One Who's always listening, Who's always hoping to hear you sing.

Lord, You are mighty, powerful, my All in All. Hear me sing—with all my heart and soul—my praises to You! Amen.

The Heart of the Matter

Only Jesus has the power to save! His name is the only one in all the world that can save anyone.

ACTS 4:12 CEV

When we want to get to "the heart of the matter," we're talking about the most important, the most critical, part of something.

When it comes to faith, Jesus is the heart of the matter. He's the most important, most critical part of our faith, the cornerstone that holds everything else up. Without Jesus, there is no point. There is no salvation, no mercy, no grace. But with Jesus we have everything and more—beyond anything you could ever imagine!

Faith must begin by believing that Jesus is Who He said—the Son of God (Matthew 3:17). You must follow Him (Matthew 4:19), obey Him (John 14:15), and lean on Him (Isaiah 41:10). You must love Him with all your heart (Luke 10:27).

Jesus is the heart of the matter. Why not let Him have yours?

Lord Jesus, this day—and every day—I give You my heart. You are everything and more to me! Amen.

A Change of Focus

*Think about the things that are good and worthy of
praise. Think about the things that are true and honorable
and right and pure and beautiful and respected.*

<small>PHILIPPIANS 4:8 NCV</small>

W here is your focus? Is it on the ugliness of the world that
scrawls across the morning headlines and the evening
news? Or is it on all the beauty and goodness and, yes, godliness
that is all around you?

Certainly the world is broken and hurting. Evil drives the
news and makes the devil smile. But there is good here too.
Open your eyes. Look for it. Each and every day, seek out
what is good and worthy of praise. Search for the things that
are right and true and honorable. Treasure those things that
are pure, full of beauty, and worthy of your respect. And,
above all, praise God for each and every one.

Stop focusing on how bad the world is and instead focus
on how good God is. Because a change of focus can make all
the difference in your world.

*Holy Father, teach me to seek out the good,
the pure, and the praiseworthy—and to
thank You for all that I find. Amen.*

Who He Created You to Be

Search me, God, and know my heart;
test me and know my anxious thoughts.
See if there is any offensive way in me,
and lead me in the way everlasting.

PSALM 139:23–24 NIV

One of the hardest questions we ask ourselves is: *What am I doing wrong?*

No one likes to be wrong, but becoming a better person is just as much about learning from our mistakes as it is about learning from our successes. And who better to ask than God, the One Who knows us inside and out? He knows what we're capable of—the best and the worst.

Examine yourself today in the mirror of God's Word. Then ask Him to search you, to show you the things you need to change. Because God knows who you are and who you should be. Humble yourself today, and let Him continue to make you who He created you to be.

Lord My God, You know me better than I know myself. Show me the things I need to change in my life so that I can be who You created me to be. Amen.

Amazed

They were all amazed at the greatness of God.

LUKE 9:43 NIV

Just a few words from Jesus sent the demon fleeing out of the boy, and the crowds were amazed. A few more words stilled the storm, and the disciples were amazed. The blind were given sight, the lame were healed, the lepers were cleansed—and the people were amazed by the greatness and power of God.

God is still amazing today. He still has the power to cast the evil and the darkness out of our lives. He still has the power to still the storms. He still has the power to restore, to heal, and to cleanse. Let the power of God pour into your life, and let Him amaze you.

Lord, You have never stopped being amazing. Please open my eyes to see Your power at work in my life and in this world. I want to be amazed by You! Amen.

The Road Ahead

You make known to me the path of life;
you will fill me with joy in your presence,
with eternal pleasures at your right hand.

PSALM 16:11 NIV

The road ahead may be bumpy or smooth, straight or winding. But it's a road that is known. No, not by you, but certainly by the One Who knows everything, Who exists outside of time. God knows every twist and turn, every hill and valley, every lurking pothole seeking to sabotage your journey.

Trust God not only to guide you home to heaven but also to help you navigate the daily pathways of a life lived here on earth. When you seek Him, God will direct your steps (Psalm 37:23). Listen and you'll hear Him softly whispering, "This is the way; walk in it" (Isaiah 30:21 NIV).

The road ahead may be filled with delights or dangers; it's impossible for you to know. But you can be absolutely sure that it's a road you'll never have to travel alone.

Lord, I trust You to know this road ahead
and to guide me on it—today, every day,
and all the way home to You. Amen.

Ask Him

*The disciples did not know what he meant. . . . They
could not understand it, and they were afraid to ask.*

LUKE 9:45 CEV

Jesus had just cast an evil spirit out of a young boy, and the crowds were amazed. But Jesus pulled His disciples aside to tell them something even more amazing: "The Son of Man is going to be betrayed into the hands of his enemies" (Luke 9:44 CEV). But take a close look at their response: *They didn't understand, and they were afraid to ask.*

Don't be afraid to ask questions of Jesus. He can handle all your questions, all your doubts and fears. And He will always answer you. It may not be what you hope to hear. It may not be immediate—you yourself may have to grow into the answer. But Jesus will always tell you the truth. So whatever that question is that you have, ask Him today.

*Lord, thank You for being a God who
welcomes my questions. And thank You for
always telling me the truth. Amen.*

JUNE 20

A Visitor in a Foreign Land

This letter is from Peter, an apostle of Jesus Christ.
"I am writing to God's chosen people who are
living as foreigners in the provinces of Pontus,
Galatia, Cappadocia, Asia, and Bithynia. . . .
"May God give you more and more grace and peace."

1 PETER 1:1–2 NLT

I f you've ever traveled to a foreign land, you know how different cultures can be: the language, the food, the traditions, the ways people celebrate and mourn. As a visitor, you want to join in—to learn the language, explore the foods and traditions. And when you're simply traveling to another country, that can be a wonderful thing.

But as a child of God, you are traveling through a foreign land—this world—every moment of your life. And while it's tempting to explore this land and its customs, and many times worthwhile, this is one land you should remain a foreigner in. Resist the language God would not have you use. Stand strong against the traditions that dismiss and dishonor Him. And turn to Him in celebration and mourning.

Lord, I don't want to fit in with the rest of the world.
Help me to resist its temptations until the day You
come and take me to my true home. Amen.

179

A Father to You

"I will be a Father to you,
And you shall be My sons and daughters,
Says the Lord Almighty."

2 Corinthians 6:18 nkjv

Perhaps you had a wonderful father, or perhaps you didn't. No earthly father is perfect, and some are much less perfect than others. But your heavenly Father is perfect in every way.

His love for you is unconditional. His patience with you is endless. And when you come to speak to Him, He is never too busy. He never says "Not now" or "In a minute." In fact, He "bends down to listen" so He can hear your every word (Psalm 116:2 nlt).

The gifts of God the Father are always good and perfectly fitted to you, "coming down from the Father of the heavenly lights, who does not change like shifting shadows" (James 1:17 niv). And the greatest of those gifts is His grace, which allows you to spend forever with Him and Him to spend forever with you.

*Holy God, You are the perfect Father, and I thank You
for all that You give me. I especially thank You for the
grace that allows me to spend forever with You. Amen.*

The One Who Never Sleeps

He who watches over you will not slumber . . .

PSALM 121:3 NIV

Sleep is a time of rest and renewal. It's necessary for our bodies to properly function. But, too often, sleep eludes us. We lay our heads down and shut off the lights, and our minds instantly spring to life, pulling up every worry, every fear, every undone must-do. What-ifs dart through the darkness like so many pesky gnats, disturbing our thoughts and keeping slumber away.

Give it all to God. Lay your head down on the pillow. Hand over all the worries, fears, must-dos, and what-ifs. You can't do a thing about them, so give them to the One Who can. Because while sleep is necessary for us, it isn't necessary for God. He never slumbers, so He can always stand watch over you, guarding you from everything—even from your own thoughts.

*Lord, when my mind will not let me sleep,
let me find rest in You. Amen.*

Jesus Prays

Therefore he is able, once and forever, to save
those who come to God through him. He lives
forever to intercede with God on their behalf.

HEBREWS 7:25 NLT

J esus spoke to His Father often. He spoke to Him in the
dark hours of night (Luke 6:12) and in the early hours of
morning (Mark 1:35). He gave thanks for His Father's provision
(John 6:11), and He begged for another way (Matthew 26:39).
In fact, it was only for that brief but eternity-changing time
upon the cross that Jesus was *not* in touch with His Father.

In other words, Jesus knows a thing or two about prayer.
So hear this truth and hold it close to your heart: *Jesus prays for
you.* Not in general, not as part of some group prayer, but personally, for *you.* It's what He returned to heaven to do. Right
this very moment, He is in the throne room of heaven pleading
for you (Romans 8:34). So when you fear you've lost your way,
when you need someone to pray for you, remember: Jesus already is.

*Lord Jesus, it is almost too wonderful
to believe that You, the King of kings,
prays for me. Thank You! Amen.*

A Gift Freely Given

It is by grace you have been saved, through faith—
and this is not from yourselves, it is the gift of
God—not by works, so that no one can boast.

EPHESIANS 2:8–9 NIV

*T*he unending goodness of God poured out on His oh-so-undeserving people. That's grace. It's for you, and for me, and for anyone who wants to claim it. God's grace doesn't have to be earned or paid for; in fact, it's impossible to do so.

Grace is "the gift of God," freely given to all who ask—to all who open their hearts to receive it. Grace isn't something we could ever achieve for ourselves—and what a blessing that is! None of us could ever make up for our sins on our own. We need God desperately . . . and that's why He gifts us with grace.

*Lord, I know that without You, without Your grace,
I am lost. Please pour Your grace down upon me
today until I am filled to overflowing. Amen.*

Surrender

"God opposes everyone
who is proud,
but he is kind to everyone
who is humble."
Surrender to God!

JAMES 4:6–7 CEV

When you've tried it your own way, fought your own battles, carved out your own path, and sought out your own solutions and failed . . . when you've halfheartedly tried it God's way and halfheartedly failed . . . when you realize there *must* be more to this life than the crushing, mindless grind . . . and when you realize that *more* lies not within our grasp but within God's . . .

. . . *let go.* Surrender to Him. Don't give up, but give in, and lean into Him.

God's got this. He calls it *grace*.

Lord, You know who I am and who I need to be. I give You my life. Make of me what You will. Amen.

More Than Words Can Say

When Moses and Elijah were leaving, Peter said,
"Master, it is good that we are here. We will put three
tents here—one for you, one for Moses, and one for
Elijah." (He did not know what he was saying.)

LUKE 9:33 ERV

P eter was perhaps the disciple whom most of us relate to best. Why? Because he always seemed to be rushing in, getting ahead of himself, and generally sticking his foot in his mouth. And this time, right after the Transfiguration, is no exception. Peter was so excited by everything he'd seen that he just had to say *something*. So he blurted out the first thing that came to mind, although it was clear that "he did not know what he was saying."

Do you ever rush to fill an awkward silence with whatever words pop into your head? Hasty words can turn an awkward silence into an instant disaster. Don't rush to speak, and don't feel as if you have to fill every silence. Slow down and ask God to sift your words. Often just being there for someone—with a smile, a hug, your presence—speaks more than words could ever say.

*Lord, guard my words today. Help me to say
only those things that are true, kind, and helpful,
and that point others right to You. Amen.*

At Just the Right Time

This is what the Lord says:
"At just the right time, I will respond to you.
On the day of salvation I will help you."

ISAIAH 49:8 NLT

Perhaps you grew tired of waiting for God's answer and tried to force your own, but the answer you found was the absolute wrong one. Maybe you found the right answer—the dream-come-true answer—at the absolute wrong time, when you didn't have the money to make a move, or when responsibilities kept you right where you were. Maybe you had the timing right—just when you needed a confirmation or a change—but the answer turned out wrong. Not that job, not that relationship, not that choice.

When we try to force it, answers and timing can be such fickle friends. But when we entrust our lives to God, we get just the right answers at just the right time. What choices can you entrust to God today, and in the future?

Lord, You know I have so little patience. It's tempting
to take things into my own hands. Please give me the
strength to wait for Your answers instead. Amen.

Unthinkable Grace

God raised us up with Christ and seated us with him in
the heavenly realms in Christ Jesus, in order that in the
coming ages he might show the incomparable riches of his
grace, expressed in his kindness to us in Christ Jesus.

EPHESIANS 2:6–7 NIV

Who would do such a thing? Who would offer unimaginable treasures to the very people who laughed in His Son's face, even though He had been sent to save them? Who would offer riches to those who arrested Him, beat Him, and crucified Him? It's unthinkable! But not to our endlessly loving God.

Our Lord offers us more grace than we could ever earn. Don't question it. Don't analyze it. And don't think too long about it.

Instead, reach out to Him. Tell Him you know Who His Son is and what He came to do. Confess to Him that you know you're sinful and lost on your own. Admit that you need Him and choose to obey Him. Then accept and embrace His unthinkable grace.

*Your grace, Lord, is unthinkable. I cannot
begin to understand it, but I am forever
grateful to You for it. Amen.*

Close to His Heart

He tends his flock like a shepherd:
He gathers the lambs in his arms
and carries them close to his heart . . .

ISAIAH 40:11 NIV

The Bible paints some of the most beautiful images of God with words that reach out to touch our hearts. In this verse from Isaiah, we see a lamb, weary, hurting, and weak . . . until the shepherd comes. He gently gathers the lamb into his arms, cradles it close to his heart, and carries it home.

Dear friend, you are the lamb, and God Himself is your shepherd. If you ever wonder what He's doing while you're weary, hurting, and weak, this is your answer. When the hours are long, the bills pile up, and love goes unreturned, God is there, ready to gather you in His arms.

Let Him.

Because then He will lift you up, cradle you close to His own heart, and carry you.

*Lord, forgive me for the times I resist You
and try to get by on my own. Please carry
me, Lord, close to Your heart. Amen.*

Grace: The Power of God

For we are God's handiwork, created in Christ Jesus to do good works, which God prepared in advance for us to do.

EPHESIANS 2:10 NIV

You were created to carry out good works for God and for His kingdom. Yes—*you.*

You, with all your fears, insecurities, and uncertainties. You, with all your questions and your doubts, with all your mess-ups, mix-ups, mistakes, and outright rebellious sins. You are God's handiwork, His one-of-kind masterpiece. His own hands crafted, molded, and shaped you with a purpose in mind—a purpose He planned long ago.

So, if you ever start to think you weren't cut out for the work He has called you to, remember this: As a child of God, you have been gifted with His grace. And that grace is the power of God at work—for you, within you, with you, and through you—transforming you and enabling you to do the good works He created you to do.

Holy Father, when I worry that I can't do the things You've called me to do, remind me of the power of Your grace working in and through me. Amen.

JULY

Stay Connected

*I am the vine; you are the branches. The one who
remains in me and I in him produces much fruit,
because you can do nothing without me.*

JOHN 15:5 CSB

G race is not a once-in-a-lifetime gift. Like the vine that
continually feeds nutrients to its branches, God's grace
will continually feed you with His life-giving strength, love,
and guidance. Because of His unending grace, He is ever working in your life—molding and shaping and making you into the
image of His own Son.

But none of that will just *happen.* You must stay connected
to the vine—to Jesus. Allow Him to prune away bad habits and
sinful ways. Spend time with Him in prayer and in His Word.
Listen to what He has to teach you. Without Him, you can do
nothing. But with Him? All things are possible!

*Holy Father, let me never wander away or
cut myself away from You. Teach me to hear
Your Words, to follow Your path, and to do
Your will—this day and always. Amen.*

In Life's Storms

"Have courage! It is I. Do not be afraid."
MARK 6:50 NCV

It had been a long, unimaginable day for the disciples. They had listened as Jesus taught, watched as He fed thousands with one boy's lunch. And now they battled a storm, alone on the sea, without Jesus. So their fear was understandable when they saw a figure walking toward them through the wind and the waves. *Walking on the water.* Then Jesus called out to them and said, "It is I. Do not be afraid."

The moment Jesus stepped into the boat, the storm stopped. Yes, they were still in that boat. And, yes, they still had to cross the sea. But they were no longer alone in the storm.

Here's the thing: You are going to have long and wearying days. You are going to be stuck in the middle of life's storms. And you are going to be afraid. In those moments—when the job is lost, the mortgage is due, and the doctor says the news is not good—close your eyes. See Him? Jesus is coming through the storm to you. And, yes, you're still in that boat. You still have to get to the other side. But you don't have to be afraid of the journey, because you are not alone.

Lord Jesus, sometimes I am so frightened by the storm. Help me realize that I am not alone. You are with me, especially in the storms. Amen.

When He Speaks

The LORD spoke the command, and the world was made.
The breath from his mouth created
everything in the heavens. . . .
[W]hen he speaks, things happen.
And if he says, "Stop!"—then it stops.

PSALM 33:6, 9 ERV

By this point in your life, you've probably learned that your own words can hold great power. But how much more power is there in the words of God? He spoke, and there was light. He spoke, and the sun, the moon, and the stars appeared. When God speaks, things happen.

And when God says, "Stop!"—everything stops. So what do you think happened when God the Son spoke the words "It is finished"? The death-grip sin held over you—over each of us—was broken. The devil's power to defeat was no more. And it *is* finished, because when God speaks, things happen.

Lord, Your words created everything in the heavens and on this earth. Your words brought life and then saved me from sin and death. I praise You, Lord, for Your words. Amen.

Let God

People are counted as righteous, not because of their work,
but because of their faith in God who forgives sinners.

ROMANS 4:5 NLT

I want to do it myself! How old are we when those words of in-dependence first spill across our lips? Two? Four? How old are we when those words stop spilling across our lips? Thirty-seven? Eighty-seven?

But the truth is we can't do it ourselves. We can't do enough good deeds or be good enough to get into heaven. We can't bridge the gulf of sin that separates us from God on our own. That's where grace comes in.

God's grace has nothing to do with our own works or our own abilities; it has everything to do with God. Set aside your independence and let God give you this gift freely. Let Him save you. Let Him give you grace.

Lord, please show me today those places
in my life where I am still trying to "do it
myself." Help me instead to depend on You,
Your strength, and Your grace. Amen.

Ripped in Two

*Then Jesus uttered another loud cry and breathed
his last. And the curtain in the sanctuary of the
Temple was torn in two, from top to bottom.*

MARK 15:37–38 NLT

Before Jesus came, a curtain separated God from His people:
a curtain woven of thread that hung in the sanctuary of
the temple, and a curtain woven of sin that hung over our lives.
But when Jesus came, that curtain began to waver in the winds
of change brought by His new covenant—a covenant of grace.

When Jesus died, all creation held its breath as the
curtain—both in the temple and in our lives—was torn in
two. It wasn't torn by human hands; it was torn from top to
bottom by God Himself, a declaration that nothing would
ever again separate His people from His love or His presence.

As you pass by a window today, notice the curtains—and
imagine God ripping apart the barrier that kept you from Him.

*Holy Father, I close my eyes and see that curtain
ripping from top to bottom. And I praise You, because
now there is nothing keeping me from You. Amen.*

The Grace of Truth

"The devil . . . has always hated the truth,
because there is no truth in him."

JOHN 8:44 NLT

The devil doesn't just like to lie; he hates the truth. And unfortunately for us, he's a very good liar. Sometimes his lies can sound dangerously like truth, especially when you are weakened by disappointment, sadness, or fear. *Unforgivable,* he'll whisper. *Unwanted. Unloved.* Like an archer targeting the bull's-eye, the devil also knows exactly where to aim his arrows to hurt you most.

When the devil whispers his lies to you, turn to the Truth of God's Word. *Unforgivable,* the devil says. *Completely forgiven,* God says (Psalm 103:12). *Unwanted,* the devil whispers. *Sought after,* God says (Luke 15:4–7). *Unloved,* the devil lies. *Endlessly and perfectly loved,* God declares (John 3:16).

Grace uses the power of God's truth to free you from the devil's lies (John 8:32). So use the truth to catch the devil in his lies—and tell him to get behind you.

*Holy Father, teach me to recognize the
devil's lies and to banish them with the grace
and power of Your Truth. Amen.*

God Will Deliver You

"I come to you in the name of the LORD of hosts, the
God of the armies of Israel, whom you have defied.
This day the LORD will deliver you into my hand . . ."

1 SAMUEL 17:45–46 NKJV

His enemy waited for him: a giant armed to the teeth, laughing at the thought of destroying him. David marched out
alone to meet Goliath. He didn't have any earthly armor or
earthly allies. His only weapon was a sling and the five smooth
stones he'd collected from the stream along the way.

But David wasn't alone: God was marching with him.
God's presence provided a heavenly armor, and God's power
made Him a divine ally. Goliath didn't destroy David that day;
rather, he himself was destroyed.

When you face down your own giants, you can know the
truth that David knew. The enemy may seem massive and
armed to the teeth, but no enemy—no liar, no betrayer, not
even the devil himself—can stand against you when you march
into battle together with God.

*Lord, when the giants in my life seem so huge
and invincible, remind me that You stand with
me and no giant can ever defeat You. Amen.*

The Heart Behind the Work

If it is not the LORD who builds a house,
the builders are wasting their time.
If it is not the LORD who watches over the city,
the guards are wasting their time.

PSALM 127:1 ERV

You can build a ministry with thousands upon thousands of followers. You can build a massive organization to feed the homeless and poor of your city. You can even build a magnificent cathedral to rival the greatest feats of architecture in the world. But if you don't build it with God as your Guard and your Guide—if you don't build it upon the foundation of His truth—then you will have wasted your time.

No matter how wonderful, how grand, or how well organized your works are, they are not eternal. It's the heart behind the work—filled with faith in the Savior, humbled before God, and seeking to always honor Him—that builds up your treasures in heaven. It isn't your works that save you; it's the faith you have in your Coworker (Ephesians 2:8–9).

Lord, the most important work I can do is to
glorify You. But no work that I do could ever
save me; only Your grace can do that. Amen.

Grace and Truth

The Word became flesh and made his dwelling among us. We have seen his glory, the glory of the one and only Son, who came from the Father, full of grace and truth.

JOHN 1:14 NIV

Grace and truth—that is what Jesus brought to us when He chose to step down from heaven to be our Rescuer, our Savior, and our Lord. Through Moses, we were given the Law, and it showed us just how sinful we really are and how short we fall of the glory of God.

But then Jesus came. And "because he was full of grace and truth, from him we all received one gift after another" (John 1:16 NCV). Grace after grace after grace was—and is—rained down upon us. When we accept His truth—that He is the Son of God and that the only way to heaven is through Him—then His grace is His gift to us. Forgiveness of sins, love unending, joy incomprehensible, mercy so undeserved . . . and grace after grace after grace.

O sweet Jesus, thank You, thank You for grace after grace after oh-so-undeserved grace. Amen.

What You Must Do

"Teacher, what must I do to get eternal life?"
LUKE 10:25 ERV

"What must I do to get eternal life?" It was a Pharisee who asked that question of Jesus, and he asked it to test Him. Jesus's answer? *Love.* And that answer hasn't changed, even though it's been more than two thousand years since Jesus first gave it.

The key to eternal life is to love the Lord with all that is in you—"'with all your heart and with all your soul and with all your strength and with all your mind'"—and "'[l]ove your neighbor as yourself'" (Luke 10:27 NIV). That kind of love is not an only-on-Sunday-morning love or an only-in-my-quiet-time love. It's not an only-for-some-people love. It's a love that colors your whole life—every word, every decision, every action. And it's a love that is impossible for you to carry out on your own.

Surrender your life to God and let Him give you that kind of love—so that you can then give it to others and back to Him again.

Lord, in this day, show me what it looks like for me to love You with all my heart, soul, mind, and strength. Amen.

Grace Tells Us When We're Wrong

The man wanted to show that the way he was living was right. So he said to Jesus, "But who is my neighbor?"

LUKE 10:29 ERV

Take a look at why the Pharisee in yesterday's story questioned Jesus in the first place: "The man wanted to show that the way he was living was right."

How often do we do the same thing? How many times do we lift up our thoughts and actions—the very ones that we know, deep down inside, are wrong—and try to justify them to God? We lay out the facts of our case before Him and expect Him to tell us we are right. But an oh-so-important part of God's grace is that He tells us when we are wrong. God won't rubber-stamp our selfishness, our pride, or our lack of love. Instead, He lovingly teaches and *reteaches* the lessons we need to learn.

What is God trying to teach you today?

Thank You, Lord, for being so patient with me. Forgive me for trying to justify my own willful ways. Guide me to fully surrender to Your ways instead. Amen.

You Do You

*Now there are [distinctive] varieties of spiritual gifts [special
abilities given by the grace and extraordinary power of
the Holy Spirit operating in believers], but it is the same
Spirit [who grants them and empowers believers].*

1 CORINTHIANS 12:4 AMP

"You do you." It's a phrase you hear quite a bit these days. And usually means something like "Do whatever it is that makes you happy." In our world, that can excuse a lot of things that don't align with the way God wants us to be. But if you apply that same phrase to your life of faith, it can be a beautiful thing.

Because God has made each of us unique, He has given each of us our own set of talents and skills. Some are visible and easily praised; others take some coaxing to uncover. But all are equally wonderful gifts from God. Don't be jealous if someone else's gift seems to shine brighter than yours, and don't be proud if yours seems to be the shinier gift. Because when you use your gifts for the glory of God—whatever that looks like—it's a wonderful thing. So, today, you do you—and celebrate all those who are out there just doing the same.

*Lord, I thank You for these gifts You've
given me. Guide me as I try to use them to
glorify You and help me to celebrate everyone
who is using their gifts for You. Amen.*

God Can!

You are strong,
and your mighty power
put the mountains in place.
You silence the roaring waves
and the noisy shouts of the nations.

PSALM 65:6–7 CEV

It's so easy to look at our own troubles and get bogged down by the impossibilities of our problems. It's so easy to see only the storm and not the Savior. It happened to Peter on the water when Jesus was literally standing right in front of him (Matthew 14:30). So how could it not happen to you every once in a while?

When the storm is all you can see, it's time to close your eyes and remember Who your God is. He's the One Who set the mountains in their places. He's the One Who silences the storms. And He's the One Who, when you call out to Him, reaches down into the waves and pulls you up to Him (Matthew 14:31).

Lord, forgive me when my eyes fill up with the wind and waves. Remind to look to You today and every day, in times of peace and in storms. I trust You to see me safely through any storm. Amen.

New Life and Relief

"LORD, you gave us new life and relief from our slavery."
EZRA 9:8 ERV

Israel had sinned against God and had been handed over to Babylonian captivity, not just as a punishment, but as a wake-up call. However, God didn't leave His people without hope. He enabled a remnant to return to their homes. He gave them "new life and relief from [their] slavery."

And He will do the same for you. When you cry out to Him, He will free you from whatever sort of prison you've landed yourself in, even when that prison is one of your own making. Because that's what God's grace does: It forgives us, lifts us up, and brings us back to Him.

*Lord, I've made mistakes, and those mistakes
have had consequences. Please forgive me and
free me from the sins of my past. Amen.*

No Fear

"The thief comes only to steal and kill and destroy; I have
come that they may have life, and have it to the full."

JOHN 10:10 NIV

What would you do for Jesus if fear and doubt weren't part of the equation? Who would you speak to? What would you give? What would you do and who would you be for Him?

The devil uses your fears like a weapon, destroying your courage, stealing your hope, and shredding your joy. Fear prevents you from sharing God's message with others, and fear keeps you from giving everything God wants you to give. Fear holds you back and scares you away from using the talents God has given you. And, perhaps worst of all, fear keeps you from believing you really are a child of God.

But all those fears are lies. Turn them over to Jesus and ask Him to shine the light of His truth through them. Don't let your fear keep you from living the abundant life Jesus came to give you.

*Lord Jesus, when fears hold me back, chase
them away with Your truth. Fill me with the
courage to do all You created me to do. Amen.*

It Began in the Garden

For the sin of this one man, Adam, caused death to rule over many. But even greater is God's wonderful grace and his gift of righteousness, for all who receive it will live in triumph over sin and death through this one man, Jesus Christ.

ROMANS 5:17 NLT

I t started in the garden so long ago, with a slippery serpent's lies and a desire to be like God. A few bites of the forbidden fruit, and sin entered the world, bringing death and separation from God along with it.

But sin wasn't the only thing that started in the garden. Grace began there too. It was grace that clothed naked sinners, and it was grace that allowed Adam and Eve to begin again after they had been cast out of the garden. It was grace that was already planning to send the Son of God to redeem all who would follow Him. Because the power of God's grace is infinitely greater than the power of sin.

Yes, sin began in the garden—but grace began there, too.

Lord, forgive me for the sins I've allowed into the garden of my own life. Please, Lord, cover and cleanse me with Your grace. Amen.

Help and Comfort

You, Lord, have helped me and comforted me.
PSALM 86:17 NCV

How valuable is receiving help when you realize you cannot do what needs to be done on your own? And how priceless is that help when it comes from the One Who has the power to move every mountain that stands in your way?

When your heart is breaking and your world seems like it's falling apart, how precious is the comfort and presence of someone who loves you? And how comforting is it if that someone is the One Who loves you perfectly, completely, and endlessly?

God is your help *and* your comfort. Call out to Him when you need Him for both these things—in big choices, in small moments, and in everything in between. He is waiting for you.

*Lord, You never fail to help and to comfort
me. Help me to show Who You are by helping
and comforting someone today. Amen.*

Keep Asking

"And so I tell you, keep on asking, and you will receive what you ask for. Keep on seeking, and you will find. Keep on knocking, and the door will be opened to you."

LUKE 11:9 NLT

Keep asking, seeking, knocking; that's the command. Jesus promises that you will receive what you ask for, you will find what you're looking for, and the door will be opened.

But you've asked and sought and knocked over and over again, and God still has not given you what you want. Didn't Psalm 37:4 promise that He would? Yes, but the key to that promise lies in the first part of the verse: *"Delight yourself also in the LORD, /* And He shall give you the desires of your heart" (NKJV; emphasis added).

God will always give you what is eternally best for you. But sometimes the things you want—the things you believe you need—aren't actually the things that are best for you. As you continue to ask, seek, and knock, God works in your heart to transform your requests until what you want matches His best . . . and this is what He gives to you.

Lord, You are the delight of my heart. Please work in me—change me—so that what I want more than anything else is for Your will to be done. Amen.

God's Got You

> "Who knows, you may have been chosen
> queen for just such a time as this."
> ESTHER 4:14 NCV

It's too difficult, too frightening, too overwhelming. It's not what you signed up for. *God,* you pray, *You are asking too much of me this day. Maybe when I'm older or wiser, or when my faith is stronger. Or maybe, Lord, You need to just find someone else.*

But God has put you in exactly the place and time He needs you to be, even if it's not the place and time you want to be in. That's what happened to Esther. But as He did with Esther, God will give you what you need to accomplish His will. "God is able to bless you abundantly, so that in all things at all times, having all that you need, you will abound in every good work" (2 Corinthians 9:8 NIV).

Perhaps it's time to help someone see how bright the light of Jesus shines in the darkness of this world. Perhaps it's time to point someone to God and to help them find the grace you've found. Whatever this time is, trust God. He's got this . . . and He's got you.

Lord, wherever You place me today, I trust
You to help me do Your will to accomplish
the plan You have for me. Amen.

A Bunch of Sinners

For all have sinned and fall short of the glory of God.

ROMANS 3:23 NKJV

As God's children, we can get so focused on the good things we're doing for God, the praises we're lifting up to Him, the time we're spending with Him, and even the blessings He rains down upon us. But sometimes we remember these things and forget who we really are: a bunch of sinners saved from the pit by the grace of God alone.

We all sin, even if we think we don't. We all fall horribly short of God's perfect standard. Not one of us deserves the blessings of heaven. Yet God, in His unending compassion, offers heaven to all of us sinners. Let that thought humble you today. Let it guide you to offer compassion to the sinners around you. And let it prompt you to praise the God Who opens heaven to sinners like you.

Lord, this day I bow before You, humbly praising and thanking You for opening heaven to me. Amen.

Anyone

Anyone can come to you,
and you will listen to their prayers.

PSALM 65:2 ERV

Absolutely *anyone* can come to God. That new mom lost in the throes of sleepless nights and endless needs. That do-whatever-it-takes-to-get-ahead person at the office. The sketchy-looking guy at the corner market. The family gossip, the waitress, the executive. You.

When the stresses of this world become too heavy, anyone can come to God and lay it all at His feet. He will give you rest from the stresses. "When our sins become too heavy for us, [He] wipe[s] them away" (Psalm 65:3 ERV). Let that truth shape your thoughts as you step out into the world today. Let it shape your words as you interact with people. Let it touch your heart as you look into the mirror. *Anyone can come to God.* And, yes, that includes you.

Lord, when I am overwhelmed with my own sins and shortcomings—or frustrated with those of others—remind me that Your grace is for anyone. I'm so grateful that "anyone" includes me. Amen.

Practice Your Faith

*The things you have learned and received and
heard and seen in me, practice these things,
and the God of peace will be with you.*
PHILIPPIANS 4:9 NASB

Almost everything we do in this world requires practice, from walking and talking to riding a bicycle and playing the tuba. We make mistakes, we learn from them, and we try again. So why would we think our walk of faith with God would be any different?

If everyone who fell off their bicycle that first time they tried to ride simply gave up and walked away, there wouldn't be any bike riders in our world. The fact is you're going to stumble in your walk of faith. You're going to make mistakes and take steps backward as well as forward. God not only knows this, but He *planned* for it. That's why He sent Jesus: to cover your mistakes with His grace.

Keep practicing your walk of faith. When you stumble, hold tight to Jesus. Get up and try again. Practice doesn't make perfect, not even when it comes to faith. But God's grace beautifully covers all your imperfections as you continue to practice your faith.

*Lord, please give me the courage, the strength,
the desire, to keep practicing the way You
want me to live. And thank You for the grace
that covers all my imperfections. Amen.*

Sin No More

"He who is without sin among you, let
him throw a stone at her first."
JOHN 8:7 NKJV

A woman is caught in the act of adultery and dragged through the streets to her punishment. Imagine you are that woman, with the taste of dirt and shame in your mouth, the sting of tears in your eyes. Feel the gravel beneath your fingers, biting into your knees as you cower before the crowd. Imagine having your worst mistakes exposed, flung out for all the world to see, to mock, to punish. You see the stones held ready. Judgment, pain, and death are waiting for you.

But this Man, the One they call Jesus, stands before the crowd and says that the one who has never sinned should throw the first stone. Confronted with their own secrets and shame, one by one the accusers leave, dropping their stones. You haven't been brought to your death after all; you've been brought to Jesus. You've been brought to new life.

Listen to the words Jesus then says, because they are for you too: "Neither do I condemn you; go and sin no more" (John 8:11 NKJV).

*Lord, You already know all my secret sins and
shames. And I know that when I ask, You forgive me.
Please, Lord, help me to sin no more today. Amen.*

A Stone's Throw

The teachers of the law and the Pharisees brought in a woman caught in adultery. They made her stand before the group.

JOHN 8:3 NIV

"Can you believe what she did?"

"I heard that he . . ."

"We should never let them get away with . . ."

How many times have you picked up a stone to throw at someone? It's so easy to judge because you know you would never fall into *that* sin. And it's so easy to join with others in condemning the one caught in the sin. But it isn't easy to do what Jesus did: standing between the one being judged and the ones holding the stones, daring to confront them with their own sins and shames. Because we all have them. All sins make us guilty before God.

The next time you find yourself facing someone caught in sin, remember that there but for the grace of God go . . . *you*. Because it's only a stone's throw between your "righteous" judgment and that sinner down in the dirt. Today, offer grace instead of stones.

Lord, forgive me for the stones I've thrown. Help me instead to offer grace and to lovingly lead sinners back to You. Amen.

What if It Is Jesus?

"Take heart; it is I."
MATTHEW 14:27 ESV

It happens to us all at one time or another. One moment, everything is sailing along smoothly, and then suddenly everything takes a turn for the worse. We veer off course.

But what if that thing that popped up out of nowhere, the thing that completely complicated your life, the thing that left you uncertain and afraid and with more questions than answers—what if that thing was Jesus's way of stepping into your life and redirecting your path to an even more glorious future?

Because sometimes the Lord shakes us up and forces us out of our comfort zones so that He can bless us with something better—something in the service of His kingdom. What if that lost job is really the first step to a much better one? What if that change in your church leads you to a closer walk with God? What if . . . ?

When chaos and upheaval seem to be ruling your day, dare to ask: *What if it's Jesus?*

Lord, when everything changes—and especially when I don't like those changes—remind me to look for You and the ways You are working in my life. Amen.

Every Single Day

Praise the Lord!
Every day he helps us with the loads we must carry.

PSALM 68:19 ERV

We all carry a load. Some are impossibly heavy: the lost job, the lost marriage, the lost loved one . . . Others are small in comparison, yet they still have the power to gather together and weigh us down: the lost keys, the lost time, the lost patience . . . And then there's the daily juggle of family and friends, work and worship.

Whatever is weighing you down today, big or small, the Lord gives you a promise: He will help you carry that load every single day. In fact, Jesus invites you to bring your burdens to Him and let Him help you carry them: "Come to me," he tells us, "and I will give you rest" (Matthew 11:28 CEV). Do you understand how amazing that promise truly is? The One strong enough to hang the sun and moon and stars in their places is offering to carry your load for you. So let Him . . . and then praise Him for it!

Lord, all these things I carry—worries, responsibilities,
endless lists of what needs to be done—I give them
to You, Lord. Guide me through them. Amen.

217

One Step Closer

Draw near to God and He will draw near to you.

JAMES 4:8 NKJV

There is so much you want to do to grow closer to God. In-depth Bible studies, exploring the original Hebrew and Greek, long prayer walks, daily journaling, and meditating upon God's Word . . . The list goes on and on.

But some days—or some seasons of life—don't allow for the extended or the in-depth. In those times, take a moment to rest in Him. Bow your heart to Him in prayer, even if your hands are too busy to be still. Choose a verse to ponder—or let a book or app choose one for you—and tuck it into your thoughts to carry with you throughout the day.

Some days allow for huge leaps in your journey with God and others for tiny steps. But even the tiniest of steps is still one step closer to Him.

Lord, I thank You for always being there, so that not only does every step I take in my faith bring me closer to You but You step closer to me as well. Amen.

When It's All About You

*For wherever there is jealousy and selfish ambition,
there you will find disorder and evil of every kind.*

JAMES 3:16 NLT

When it's all about you—when your words and thoughts all seem to begin with "I" or "me," or when your frustrations are focused on the things you didn't get but someone else did—that's when it might be time to check for a little condition of the heart known as *selfishness*.

Selfishness is at the root of just about every sin. Simply put, it's placing your own desires over the desires of others—even God's. And while the world will tell you it's perfectly okay to go after what you want, God has a different way for you to live: "Try to do what is good for others, not just what is good for yourselves" (1 Corinthians 10:24 ERV). This *unselfish* way of living is a kind of grace you can give to the world around you.

How can you give unselfishly to someone today?

*Lord, selfishness slips into my life so easily, just a bit
at a time. Show me the ways I am being selfish today,
and help me to choose unselfishness instead. Amen.*

Why Worry?

Can all your worries add a single moment to your life?
And if worry can't accomplish a little thing like that,
what's the use of worrying over bigger things?
LUKE 12:25–26 NLT

Worry is practically a staple of life in our society. But what good does worrying really do us? How much of your life has been wasted on worrying about things that never even happened? And of the things that did happen, did worry really help at all? Your Heavenly Father knows absolutely everything that's happening in your life—not just yesterday and today, but also what will happen tomorrow. "Every day of my life was recorded in your book," Psalm 139:16 (NLT) tells us. "Every moment was laid out / before a single day had passed." God's already got a plan for how to walk with you.

The fact is, worry is really a fear of not being in control—and you aren't. But you know the One Who is. He loves you so much, He gave up His own Son for you (John 3:16). So close your eyes for a moment, tuck those worries into a box, seal it up tight, and give it to Him. Then take His hand and step into the day, without fear or worry, trusting Him every step of the way.

Lord, I know that You love me, and I know that You
are in control. Help me to trust You, Lord, with all these
things I worry about—and then to not worry. Amen.

Enough to Make It Beautiful

"If God makes what grows in the field so beautiful,
what do you think he will do for you? That's just
grass . . . But God cares enough to make it beautiful.
Surely he will do much more for you."
LUKE 12:28 ERV

Have you ever contemplated all the things in this world that God has made beautiful? He didn't have to invest that much effort into the richly vibrant colors on the petals of a flower—and not just the rose, but even the blooms of the most common of weeds. He didn't have to put so much detail into sculpting that faraway star that we've only just developed the technology to see.

But God cares enough to include beauty in the tiniest of details, and He cares enough to insert beauty into every moment of your life as well. You just need to open your eyes to see it. As you listen to the laughter of a child, hear the delight of God. As you hold the hand of the one you love, feel the warmth of God envelop you. And, yes, even as you stand in the rain at a graveside, feel the comforting kiss of His tears on your brow. God's beautiful details are present in every day of your life; you just have to look for them.

*Lord, I thank You for the beauty You instill in
my life. Open my eyes to see it, Lord, and my
heart to feel it and praise You for it! Amen.*

Neck Deep

God, save me from all my troubles!
The rising water has reached my neck.
I have nothing to stand on.
I am sinking down, down into the mud.
I am in deep water,
and the waves are about to cover me.

PSALM 69:1–2 ERV

Have you ever felt as David did in this Psalm: already up to your neck in water, with the waves rising fast? About to drown in worry, fear, debt, illness, sin, sadness, busyness, or even hatred? Do as David did: Cry out to God in prayer to rescue you "from the mire" of your situation (Psalm 69:13–14 NIV).

And then praise Him, as David did, for the answer you can be sure is coming. In His perfect time and way, God will lift out of the muddy waters. He will be with you "in trouble" to "deliver [you] and honor [you]" (Psalm 91:15 NIV). He will rescue you.

*Lord, when I feel overwhelmed and up to my
neck in rising waters, remind me that You
are the God who rescues. Give me courage
as I wait for You to save me. Amen.*

AUGUST

Beautifully Broken

*He heals the brokenhearted
and binds up their wounds.*

PSALM 147:3 NIV

You are the creation of God's own hands, masterfully and wonderfully made. But life has a way of chipping away at us little by little. It gives us a nagging sense that we're just not good enough—whether it comes from a parent who is never pleased or because we are overwhelmed by a too-long to-do list.

And then sometimes life steps in to land a heavy blow and shatters us in the form of illness, loss, or even betrayal. What do you do with all those chipped-away parts of yourself, those broken pieces that no longer seem to fit together?

Give them to God. Let Him take them, cover them in His love, and bind them together with His grace so that the new whole that emerges is stronger than ever—made even more beautiful by the brokenness.

*Lord, I pray that You will take all these
broken bits and pieces of me and mend me.
Make me whole again in You. Amen.*

Sight to the Blind

"I entered this world to render judgment—to give sight to the blind and to show those who think they see that they are blind."

JOHN 9:39 NLT

The man had been blind since birth. He'd never seen a thing—not a flower, not a sunrise, not his own mother's face—until Jesus came. Jesus healed the man and gave him eyes that saw. But that man saw more than just the flowers, the sunrise, and his mother's face (John 9:30). He saw Jesus and recognized Him as the Son of God (John 9:35–38).

The Pharisees, on the other hand, whose hardened hearts were angered by Jesus's gift to the blind man, didn't see a thing. They didn't see that Jesus's healing was more important than the traps they were trying to set for Him. They didn't see that grace trumped judgment. And they didn't see that Jesus was the Son of God.

God's grace enables the spiritually blind to see, but He won't force you to open your eyes. You have to trust Him enough to look.

*Lord, I know there are times when I have been
blind to Your grace, Your truth, Your will.
Open my eyes, Lord. I want to see! Amen.*

When God Moves In

"My Father is always working, and so am I."

JOHN 5:17 NLT

God is always with you. He never leaves your side, not even for a moment. He is usually in the quiet whispers, the peaceful corners of your heart, and the stillness of your thoughts. But sometimes God works in big and bold ways—powerful, visible, obvious, and undeniable.

There will be moments when God will move into the forefront of your life in dramatic ways that change everything. He may have already done so in your life. Just ask Moses about the time he saw that burning bush, or Mary about that time the angel appeared, or Paul about what he witnessed on the road to Damascus.

When God moves in, everything changes. Look for the ways—big and bold, or still and small—that He's moving in your life today.

Holy Father, I know You are always with me, always working in my life. Teach me to see You, Lord, and to welcome You in all the ways You work. Amen.

A Change in Perspective

We do not look at the things which are seen, but at the things which are not seen. For the things which are seen are temporary, but the things which are not seen are eternal.

2 CORINTHIANS 4:18 NKJV

Perspective can change everything. When you're in the midst of the hustle and bustle of your world, small things can seem big, big things can seem huge, and the huge things can become completely overwhelming. Earthly to-do lists, bills, cleaning, cooking, and organizing your life seem so much more urgent than eternal tasks like caring, encouraging, giving, and sharing.

When the urgent outweighs the eternal in your life, it's time for a change in perspective. Stop, drop to your knees, and pray. Because when you stop looking out at everything you need to do and start looking up to God, your perspective changes, your priorities shift, and the eternal becomes essential once again.

Lord, let me never mistake the earthly for the eternal. Keep my life, my heart, and my hands focused on serving You. Amen.

Words

Set a guard, O LORD, over my mouth; Keep
watch over the door of my lips.

PSALM 141:3 NKJV

Words can be more trouble than they're worth, especially when they rush out of our mouths unchecked by our hearts and our minds. Whether it's in the heat of anger or because of the sting of impatience, the words we speak in haste to get our point across can get us into all kinds of trouble.

Slow down today. When you feel the words piling up and preparing to spill out, send up a quick prayer to heaven: "LORD, help me control my tongue; / help me be careful about what I say" (Psalm 141:3 NCV). Because words don't just have the propensity to harm others; they can also be mighty tools in the kingdom of God—when you allow Him to control them.

Lord, guard my words. Let only those that are pleasing to You slip past my lips today. Amen.

Our Father

"Our Father in heaven . . ."
MATTHEW 6:9 NIV

When Jesus's disciples asked Him to teach them to pray, He began His prayer with these words: "Our Father in heaven . . ."

It was a prayer lifted up to God the Father by God the Son, Who willingly left heaven to walk beside His people on earth, to lead them and to guide them. And it is a prayer that continues today as God the Spirit—Who now lives *within* His people—lifts up prayers on our behalf to our Father in heaven.

Do you see the circle of unending prayer and unfailing love that envelopes you? Step into the prayers of God the Father, the Son, and the Spirit. Allow them to embrace and enfold you. Step into that love, and be filled with the grace of "our Father in heaven."

Holy Father, I praise You for the prayers you have taught me to pray and for the prayers Your Son and Your Spirit unceasingly lift up for me. Amen.

Less Than Perfect

*I am certain that God, who began the good work
within you, will continue his work until it is finally
finished on the day when Christ Jesus returns.*

PHILIPPIANS 1:6 NLT

You don't have to get it right every time. You're allowed to make mistakes. God knows you're human, and He's not finished with you yet—so you can stop worrying about being perfect.

Don't give up on yourself or on God's promises. The mistakes you make won't cost you His love. Your shortcomings won't cast you out of His presence. Not even your outright sins could rob you of His grace.

So when you fall on your face, get up and fall on your knees. Go to God and confess that you know you've made mistakes. And then accept His amazing gift of grace. After all, it's why He sent His Son: to be perfect so that you don't have to be afraid when you're less than perfect.

*Holy Father, I make so many mistakes. Forgive
me. And when I fall, remind me that Your
love and grace are still there for me. Amen.*

Mirrors

You are altogether beautiful . . .
SONG OF SONGS 4:7 NIV

The mirror over the sink likes to point out all your imperfections. The mirror of the media will tell you that you're not important unless you own this, wear this, drive this, do this. And the mirror of the world will scream that, in the scheme of things, you're nothing at all. Even the mirrors of family and friends can be distorted, reflecting back the person they want you to be.

There is only one true mirror that never lies, and only one that shows you exactly who you really are: the mirror of God's Word. Look into it to see who you really are: the "wonderfully made" (Psalm 139:14 NIV), altogether beautiful child of God (1 John 3:1).

Holy Father, when I look into the mirror—the one on the wall and the one in Your Word— help me to see myself as You see me. Amen.

Be Honest with Yourself

The LORD . . . delights in those who tell the truth.
PROVERBS 12:22 NLT

Honesty is a foundational part of the Christian faith. "You shall not give false testimony against your neighbor" is even one of the Ten Commandments (Exodus 20:16 NIV). But there's more to being honest than not lying to others; we also have to make sure we aren't lying to ourselves, or to God.

It takes more than a little courage to admit your own weaknesses and shortcomings. But being honest enough with yourself to admit what you need also gives you the humility to accept it. We need God's grace.

Be honest with God. Seek Him, confessing that He is the only One Who can save you; He promises to be found (Jeremiah 29:13). And accept His grace: It's yours for the asking.

Lord, if I want to find my home in You, then I know I cannot live this life on my own. I'm so grateful to You that I never have to. Amen.

The Nearness of God

We praise you, God!
We praise you because you are near to us.

PSALM 75:1 ERV

When you're frightened, having someone near helps you face your fears. Sorrows are made more bearable by having a friend by your side, and joys become even more joyful when you have someone to share them with. In Ecclesiastes 4:9–12, Solomon said that "two are better than one" (ERV) because they can lift one another up, keep each other warm, and stand strong against any enemy.

There may be times when you feel alone, but God is always nearby to strengthen you, to comfort you, and to share in your joys. His presence is with you wherever you go, whatever you do. God is never more than the breath of a whispered prayer away.

Holy Father, I praise You for Your constant
presence in my life, for lifting me up, for keeping
me in the warmth of Your love, and for standing
strong with me against the enemy. Amen.

The Little Children

One day some parents brought their little children to Jesus
so he could touch and bless them. But when the disciples
saw this, they scolded the parents for bothering him.
Then Jesus called for the children and said to the disciples, "Let
the children come to me. Don't stop them! For the Kingdom
of God belongs to those who are like these children."
LUKE 18:15–16 NLT

A group of parents bring their children to Jesus, but the disciples scold them and shoo them away. How does Jesus react? Yes, Jesus calls the children to come back to Him, but then *He scolds the disciples*, telling them, "Let the children come to me. Don't stop them!" Why? Because "the Kingdom of God belongs to those who are like these children." Jesus made it clear that He could never be too busy for His children.

Now consider this: When you decide to follow Jesus, you become one of God's little children. He is never too busy for you and He will never send you away. God is the God of the entire universe, but you are never, ever a nuisance to Him. Day or night, when you come to Jesus, He opens His arms, gathers you close, and blesses you with His love.

Holy Lord Jesus, let me come to You as
a little child, telling You everything and
following wherever You lead. Amen.

A Foundation for Life

Anyone who hears and obeys these teachings of mine is like a wise person who built a house on solid rock. Rain poured down, rivers flooded, and winds beat against that house. But it did not fall, because it was built on solid rock.

MATTHEW 7:24–25 CEV

Have you ever stood at the edge of the ocean, your toes planted firmly in the sand? What happens as the waves wash over your feet? The sand slips away beneath you and you begin to sink. Small waves steal only a few grains of sand, but huge, crashing waves leave you off-balance, reeling, and trying not to fall.

That's a lot like what happens in life when you try to stand on the promises of fame, success, money, or self-righteousness. Even wonderful things like families and friendships can falter, leaving you struggling for balance. Build your life on God instead. Let Him be the foundation of your life. He never shifts or changes; instead, He is always faithful to love and will help you.

Holy Father, it's so tempting to put my faith in things like career, money, family, or friends. But I know that You are the only One Who lasts, the only One Who will never fail me. I will build my life on You. Amen.

The Road to Follow

Trust in the LORD with all your heart
and lean not on your own understanding;
in all your ways submit to him,
and he will make your paths straight.
PROVERBS 3:5–6 NIV

These verses from Proverbs 3 are some of the most memorized and quoted of the Bible, and for good reason. They contain a beautiful promise: If you trust God and seek His will instead of your own, He will show you the way to go.

We're desperate to know if we're heading in the right direction in our lives. But what does that look like on an average Tuesday morning, or Friday afternoon, or Saturday night? Does it mean that God will show you every move to make, from the second you get out of bed to the moment you crawl back into it? No. But it does mean that, with every step you take, you think about what God wants you to do. You trust the wisdom of His Word for guidance. You may not understand why you should forgive that person, serve that group, or give your time away. But when you do, God will not only show you which road to follow; He will clear it before you.

*Lord, I am so often tempted to barge through my days,
doing what I want. Remind me to stop and consider
what You want—and then to do that instead. Amen.*

The Hands of God

He reached down from heaven and rescued me;
he drew me out of deep waters.

PSALM 18:16 NLT

Stop for a moment and think about the hands of God. His hands laid the very foundations of the earth and spread out the heavens above it (Isaiah 48:13). God has "held the oceans in his hand" and "measured off the heavens with his fingers" (Isaiah 40:12 NLT). He can gather the winds up in His fists (Proverbs 30:4). He took the dust of the earth, shaped it into a man, and called him Adam.

The hands of God move mountains and scatter stars, yes—but these same hands have also reached down from heaven and stretched out to clasp yours. His grip is firm and sure, and you know He will never let you go. His hands lift you up out of the deep waters of sin and death and cradle you close to His heart.

Lord, I praise You for the power of Your hands and for
the wonders You have done with them. But most of all
I thank You for using Your hands to rescue me. Amen.

For Your Own Good

If you forgive others for the wrongs they do to you,
your Father in heaven will forgive you. But if you don't
forgive others, your Father will not forgive your sins.

MATTHEW 6:14–15 CEV

Over and over again the New Testament repeats the message that if you want to be forgiven of your sins, you must also forgive those who sin against you. Every letter of God's Word is important, but when God repeats Himself, it's time to sit up and pay extra attention to what He has to say.

And God talks *a lot* about forgiveness: Be forgiving (Ephesians 4:32), forgive seventy times seven times (Luke 17:3–4), and forgive because you've been forgiven (Colossians 3:13). Why does God stress the importance of forgiveness so often? He forgave us so that we could pass that forgiveness on to others. And He knows that holding on to your anger leads to bitterness and keeps you from experiencing the good things He has planned for you to do (James 1:20).

So, today, forgive those who wrong you—for your own sake and because God forgives you, over and over again.

Lord, if there is any unforgiveness lurking in my heart
today, help me to rid myself of it and make it right. Amen.

Otherwise Impossible

I can do all things through Christ who strengthens me.

PHILIPPIANS 4:13 NKJV

Philippians 4:13 is a powerful verse, but it is often misused. It does not mean that God will give you the strength and ability to do whatever *you* want. If you're a five-foot-three-inch klutz dreaming of playing professional basketball, Philippians 4:13 is probably not going to be your answer.

But this verse does promise that God will help you do all things that are *His* will for your life. God will help you learn to be content in times of both want and plenty (Philippians 4:12). God will help you find joy even in the midst of trials and suffering (James 1:2). When you turn to God for strength and guidance, He enables you to do the truly amazing—and otherwise impossible—work of shining the light of His love into this dark world. Talk to God today. Ask Him to show you what impossible thing He wants to make possible for you.

Lord, You are the One Who gives me the strength and the courage to do all that I do. Help me, Lord, to do even more—with You and for You. Amen.

Absolutely Amazing!

I will praise You, for I am fearfully and wonderfully made;
Marvelous are Your works,
And that my soul knows very well.
PSALM 139:14 NKJV

If you were asked to describe yourself, what words would spring to mind? Would you say you're *okay*, or *pretty good*, or perhaps *not too bad, considering*?

But what words does God use to describe you? The author of the Psalm knows that you are *fearfully* (as in "awe-inspiring") and *wonderfully made*. Why do we shy away from claiming how awesome we are? This doesn't mean thinking *I'm better than you* but rather that we—each and every one of us, individually—are absolutely amazing.

Just think about the complexity of your body, of what it takes to do the simple task of reading this page—eyes scanning the text, hand holding the book, mind pondering the words while your heart beats, your blood pumps, and your lungs inhale. And that's just your body. You also have a heart that loves, a mind that ponders, and a soul that lives forever. *You*—body, mind, and soul—are absolutely amazing.

Lord, I praise You for fearfully, wonderfully, and marvelously making me! Help me to tell the world how fearfully, wonderfully, and marvelously amazing You are. Amen.

Add to Your Asking

"If you believe, you will receive whatever you ask for in prayer."

MATTHEW 21:22 NIV

Have you ever found yourself thinking, *Lord, I do believe, but . . . ?* Because you've been praying, and you've been believing, yet you still haven't received. Why would God withhold His gifts from you?

Sometimes we don't receive the things we ask for because we haven't been obeying God's Word as we should (1 John 3:21–22). Ask God to show you if there is sin in your life and to help you rid yourself of it.

But difficult times don't mean that God is punishing us. Other times, the thing we are asking for is simply not God's will for us (1 John 5:14–15). Perhaps the thing we want is something He knows will harm us, or perhaps He has something better planned for us. Keep praying, asking God to shape your will until it matches His own.

When God doesn't seem to be answering your prayers, don't give up. Don't stop believing. Don't stop asking. God will answer.

Lord, You know the things I want and the things I believe I need. But I trust You. Change my prayers until they match Your will. Amen.

Expectations

God is the one I am trying to please.

GALATIANS 1:10 ERV

You family expects certain things from you. Friends expect others. Then there's church, and school, and work and . . . and . . . and you're just so tired.

The weight of the world's expectations can be crushing. But perhaps the most crushing expectations are the ones you put on yourself: that you have to do everything, be everything, and succeed at everything. You don't, dear one. You don't.

Don't let expectations—from others or from yourself— crush you. Carry them to Jesus and let Him share the weight. He tells us that if we come to Him with our burdens, He will give us rest (Matthew 11:28). Search out God's expectations for you. Ask Him to sort through each of your burdens. Let Him show you what is truly important, what can wait, and what can simply be put down. Seek to please God, and everything else will fall into place.

Lord, please help me to worry less about what others expect and to simply seek to please You with all I do and say. Amen.

What Can I Do for You?

"Seek the Kingdom of God above all else, and
he will give you everything you need."
LUKE 12:31 NLT

So often we come to God with our lists of demands, requests, and pleas. *I need You to do this for me. Could You
fix this for me? Please, Lord . . .*

There's nothing inherently wrong with this. God Himself
has given us access to the very throne room of heaven in order
to lay our prayers before Him "with confidence" (Hebrews
14:16 NIV). We should ask Him for the things we want and need
"in every situation" (Philippians 4:6 NIV). He invites you to
"pour out your hearts to him" (Psalm 62:8 NIV) and to "cast all
your anxiety on him because he cares for you" (1 Peter 5:7 NIV).

But when we come to God with only our own vision in
mind of how things should be, we miss out on the incredible
possibilities, opportunities, and blessings that God has in store
for us. So try something different today. Carry your requests
to God and leave them in His perfect care, but then ask this
one simple question: *What can I do for You today, Lord?*

*Lord, You do so much for me—so much I don't
even realize You're doing it. So today, Lord, I ask
You to show me what I can do for You. Amen.*

A Picture of Grace

Surely your goodness and love will follow me
all the days of my life,
and I will dwell in the house of the LORD
forever.

PSALM 23:6 NIV

They say a picture is worth a thousand words, but some words—especially those inspired by our Heavenly Father—are worth more than a thousand pictures. If you've ever wondered what grace looks like, Psalm 23 paints the picture.

Grace is the loving Shepherd Who makes sure you want for nothing. He gives you the peace of green pastures to refresh your world-weary soul and quiet waters to ponder by.

Grace guides you when you don't know which way to go, walks with you through the darkness, and lifts you up above the reach of your enemies. It protects and shields, loves and blesses endlessly.

God is grace. And when you choose to follow Him, His goodness follows you all the days of your life—and forever more.

*Lord, You pour so much grace into my life,
and I praise You for every drop. Remind
me that You are grace, Lord. Amen.*

Look Up

I lift up my eyes to the mountains—
where does my help come from?
My help comes from the LORD,
the Maker of heaven and earth.

PSALM 121:1–2 NIV

*W*hen you're lost, look up. That's good advice for travelers. Because when you're out on the sidewalk of a big city, all those buildings start to look alike. And when you're in a forest full of trees, all that bark tends to look the same. So look up to search out a landmark to guide the way.

Why should it be any different for our spiritual lives? When you're lost, look up to God. When you're out in the world, all those choices can start to look the same. Sometimes there is no clear-cut choice, but even right and wrong don't look as different as they should when they're painted in all those shades of gray. So look up to God: He'll be your landmark. You can navigate His path if your eyes are fixed on Him.

Lord, as I walk through the world today, remind
me to look up to You every so often and make
sure I'm headed the right way. Amen.

Don't Be Afraid

"Don't be afraid; just believe . . ."
LUKE 8:50 NIV

Have you ever noticed how many times the Lord tells someone not to be afraid? "Do not be afraid," the angel told Hagar in the desert (Genesis 21:17 NIV). "Do not be afraid of them," God told Joshua as he battled through the Promised Land (Joshua 10:8 NIV). "Take courage! It is I. Don't be afraid," Jesus told His disciples as He walked toward them on the water (Matthew 14:27 NIV). Jesus spoke these words to His disciples, to Peter, to Jairus . . . and, through His Word, God says it to you.

Perhaps that's because God understands just how frightening this world can be. But over and over again, God reassures you: You don't have to be afraid. God is always with you, even when all seems lost. He is always fighting for you. And He is always there to guide you through any storm. The gift of His grace means you don't ever have to be afraid.

Lord, this world is filled with frightening things, but not one of them is bigger, stronger, or more powerful than You. I will trust You and not be afraid today. Amen.

Blessed to Believe

"Blessed are you when people hate you,
when they exclude you and insult you
and reject your name as evil,
because of the Son of Man."

LUKE 6:22 NIV

Sometimes, saying you are a child of God can feel like painting a target on your chest, inviting misunderstanding and ridicule. Some will call you misguided; some will assume that you're foolish and naïve. Some people will assume you are unkind. You may lose out on opportunities, friendships, or family relationships when you choose to faithfully follow God. And sometimes following God looks different from what even fellow Christians expect it to look like.

The temptation to "give up" on believing in God can be very real, but don't surrender to it. Remember, this world hated Jesus, who was a perfect reflection of His Father. How could it feel any less hatred for you? Don't give up. Keep believing in the One Who never gives up on You—and He will bless you.

*Lord, I lift up to You all those who hate Your people.
Work in their hearts, show them who You are,
and help them to believe in You too. And help me
follow Your path even when it's difficult. Amen.*

Love and Do and Be

It is through him that we are able to live, to
do what we do, and to be who we are.

ACTS 17:28 ERV

When Paul arrived in Athens, he found himself surrounded by idols. The people worshipped so many different gods that they even had an idol "to an unknown god" (Acts 17:23 ERV) so that they wouldn't unknowingly leave out or offend a god who needed their worship.

When you step out into the world, you will likely find yourself surrounded by idols—a different sort of idol, but no less worshipped with time and money and attention. For some, it's relationships. For others, it's a career. It can be family, friendships, sports, yourself, money . . . An idol is anything that becomes more important than God.

Ask God to show you the idols in your life and help you return your worship to Him. Live for Him and His glory. For it is only by His grace that you live with the hope and promise of heaven.

Lord, show me the idols in my life and
help me to get rid of them. I want You to
be the only God of my life. Amen.

God Is with You

If God is for us, no one can stand against us. And God is with us.
ROMANS 8:31 ERV

Why do we so often doubt God's presence in our lives? God has torn down the curtain of sin that kept His people separated from Him (Matthew 27:51). He's sent His very own Spirit to make His home inside you (Romans 8:11). He didn't even spare His own Son but gave Him up for you (Romans 8:32). Is there anything good this God will not give you? Is there anything He would not do to save you?

The Lord of All Creation is on your side, guiding you, defending you, covering you with the righteousness of His own Son. Now, *that* is grace—undeniable and amazing grace.

Lord, I am so thankful You are with me. I will trust You to guide me, defend me, and cover me with Your grace. Amen.

Sing and Celebrate

I will sing about
your strength, my God,
and I will celebrate
because of your love. . . .
I will sing your praises!

PSALM 59:16–17 CEV

D avid's words in Psalm 59 call to mind images of joyful days
filled with love and laughter and blessings.

But the reality of David's situation when this psalm was
written was far from joyful. Instead of love, there was hatred.
Instead of laughter, there was cursing. And instead of blessings,
there were the threats and lies of his enemies. These beautiful
words were written when Saul had set David in his sights to kill
him. And yet David found a reason to sing and celebrate God.

What does that tell you about your own songs, about your
own reasons to celebrate? God doesn't just deserve praise for
what He's done for you, for your own circumstances; God deserves praise for who He is.

*Lord, I will praise You in the joy-filled times and
in the difficult times. I will praise You always,
for the grace You always give me. Amen.*

Make the Days Count

Teach us to number our days,
That we may gain a heart of wisdom.

PSALM 90:12 NKJV

S omeone once said that the days are long but the years are short. Each day can stretch out endlessly in a blur of things to do, places to be, bills to pay, dishes to wash, projects to pull together. But at the end of the day, you wonder where the hours went. At the end of the week, you wonder where the days went. Then suddenly you blink, and twenty years have slipped away.

Time is so easily lost in the mundane daily tasks of life, but we shouldn't settle for that. Seek joy in the days God gives you. Notice the millions of tiny blessings He sprinkles into your days: the glisten of raindrops, the calls of birds, the smile of a friend. Celebrate His gifts. Celebrate *Him. Share Him.* Don't count the days; instead make the days count.

Lord, teach me to see Your gifts in the everyday
wonders of this life You've gifted me with.
And help me to share You—the greatest gift
of all—with those around me. Amen.

The Power of Grace

"I am sending you out like sheep among wolves. Therefore be as shrewd as snakes and as innocent as doves."

<small>MATTHEW 10:16 NIV</small>

Jesus sent His disciples out into a rough world with the above verse to guide their behavior: "as shrewd as snakes and as innocent as doves." He was telling the disciples to be aware of the sin and evil that those around them were plotting, but not to have any part of it. That's good advice for today too, because the world Jesus is sending you out into is just as rough, though perhaps in different ways.

Jesus sends you out not only with His advice but also with His blessing and His grace. That grace is more than a promise to forgive and to save. It's the power of Christ Himself at work in your life to guide and to guard you—and it's His grace that covers you completely as you step out into the world today.

Lord, teach me to recognize the evil and sin that is around me. And please give me the strength to stay away from it. Amen.

The Blessings of Heaven

"Where your treasure is, there your heart will be also."
LUKE 12:34 NKJV

Have you ever started to give—of your time, your money, your possessions—and then stopped yourself, thinking, *But I might need this for myself?* Our world encourages you to rely on yourself, but as a child of God, you can—and should—rely on Him. God knows the things you need, and He promises to provide for you (Luke 12:22–31). And because God will provide what you need, you can give, generously and without fear.

You can give up your earthly treasures because they are *nothing* compared to the heavenly treasures you are gathering when you give. It's like trading a copper penny for a vault full of gold. Giving is one thing God asks us to test Him with: Give and He will pour out the blessings of heaven upon you (Malachi 3:10). Because you have been given grace, you can give to others. Ask God to show you where and how you can give today.

Lord, it is hard to give sometimes, whether it's because of selfishness or fear. Help me to trust You to provide what I need—and then to give without fear. Amen.

Assume the Best

God showed how much he loved us by sending
his one and only Son into the world so that we
might have eternal life through him.

1 JOHN 4:9 NLT

We don't tend to assume the best in every situation, do we? Sometimes every slight seems intentional, every hurt premeditated, every word and action carefully crafted to cut us.

Why do we so often assume the worst of others? Could it be that, deep down, we believe that we aren't really worthy of people's best? Could we think that we deserve the bad things that happen to us? The next time you find yourself assuming the worst, consider this: The God of All Creation—the One Who knows you inside and out—gave you His Son and His grace. He gave you His very best.

*Lord, I am so far from perfect, yet You believe I am
worth Your best. Help me to give others my best—
and to assume they are doing the same. Amen.*

SEPTEMBER

Shine

"When you look at people and want to help them,
you are full of light. But when you look at people
in a selfish way, you are full of darkness."

LUKE 11:34 ERV

When you have a light in a dark place, you don't hide it. You hold it up high to help others see (Luke 11:33). You have been given the light of the truth of Jesus, and with the Holy Spirit working within you, you have been given the power to lift up this light for all the world to see. But what does that really mean? What does it look like when you step out into the world?

It's all about how you see the world and the people around you. If you look at another person and only see what you think is wrong with them or how you can use them for your own gain, then you are hiding your light under a bowl. But if you see someone and seek to help them, you are shining your light—the light of Jesus—into the world. It really is that simple. So go out and shine today!

Lord, help me not to selfishly hide away this
light You've given me but rather to lift it up
so that others can better see You. Amen.

God Has Plans for You

"For I know the plans I have for you," says the
LORD. "They are plans for good and not for
disaster, to give you a future and a hope."

JEREMIAH 29:11 NLT

God has big, bold, and amazing plans for you. But here's the thing: God's plans for your life may not match yours. And they may not be so wonderful according to this world's standards. After all, God's perfect plan for His own Son involved leaving heaven and being arrested, beaten, and crucified on a cross.

The key to trusting God's plans for your life is this: Every plan that God had for His Son—and every plan that He has for you—is thoughtfully and carefully designed to accomplish His ultimate goal. God will bring you home to heaven to live with Him one day, and He will use you to bring others home to Him too. Because God doesn't want to spend eternity without you.

*Lord, I will confess that there are times when
Your plans are hard for me to follow. Please
help me remember and trust Your ultimate
plan—to get me home to You. Amen.*

Knowing God

*"Those who wish to boast
should boast in this alone:
that they truly know me and understand that I am the LORD
who demonstrates unfailing love
and who brings justice and righteousness to the earth,
and that I delight in these things."*

JEREMIAH 9:24 NLT

So often we turn to God when we don't know what to do—and He's certainly the One Who knows all things. But don't just seek God for the answers He provides, the strength He offers, or the blessings He gives. Seek God simply to get to know Him. Because, as amazing as it seems, the God of All Creation wants a relationship with you.

Read His Word and notice the way He loves His people even when they don't love Him. See how He steps in to help, to guide, to save. Carve out the time to build a relationship with Him. Because spending time with God—whether it's in prayer or in His Word—isn't just about knowing what to do. It's about knowing God.

*Holy Father, You know everything there is to know
about me. Show me who You are today. Amen.*

A Gentle Nudge

"I will ask the Father to send you the Holy Spirit who will
help you and always be with you. The Spirit will show you
what is true. The people of this world cannot accept the
Spirit, because they don't see or know him. But you know
the Spirit, who is with you and will keep on living in you."
JOHN 14:16–17 CEV

You've felt it before: that gentle nudge leading you to give
to the homeless man you would have ordinarily ignored.
That quiet whisper prompting you to call that friend you hadn't
planned to call or urging you to speak when you would really
rather have stayed silent. That's the Spirit of God nudging you
to be His hands and His feet.

Or perhaps you felt that gentle nudge stopping you from
doing something that you had planned to do, a check in your
heart that said, *Don't step through that door, don't trust that person, don't believe that lie.* That's the Spirit of God too, guiding
and protecting you.

Today, keep yourself open to the gentle nudges of God's
Spirit; they are part of His gift of grace.

*Lord, I'm afraid that so often I miss Your
gentle nudges. Teach me to be more attentive
to the leadings of Your Spirit in me. Amen.*

A Prayer to Lead Me

Teach me to do your will,
for you are my God;
may your good Spirit
lead me on level ground.

PSALM 143:10 NIV

Lord, there is so much swirling around in my mind: what to do or not to do, what to say or to keep quiet, which path to take, how to repair this relationship . . . The thoughts go on and on. But most of all, I fear that I am not being the person You created me to be.

Sift through my heart, Lord. Show me the things I do that bring honor to Your name and the things I do that break Your heart. Help me to purge the hurtful things from my life and cultivate the healthy ones. Lead me so that each word, each step, each thought, glorifies You today.

And to all this, Lord, I say, "Amen."

Holy Father, I pray that You will teach me Your ways. Show me how I should live each moment of this day. Amen.

When Words Aren't Enough

I thought about you, God,
and tried to tell you how I felt, but I could not.

PSALM 77:3 ERV

The right words can be hard to find at times: in front of a crowd, when you're nervous or excited, and even in your prayers to God.

Because sometimes the emotions are just too big. The joy, the anger, and the despair can be too overwhelming to capture in words. Your thoughts jump around, your heart overflows, and the words get stuck somewhere between your mind and your tongue. You need to tell God what's happening in your life, but the right words just won't come.

It's okay. Breathe. Be still before God. Let the Spirit settle your thoughts and lift you up to the Father. He'll speak for you when words just aren't enough, because when "we do not know what we ought to pray for . . . the Spirit himself intercedes for us through wordless groans" (Romans 8:26 NIV).

Father, I thank You for the gift of Your Spirit, Who
speaks for me when I cannot speak for myself. Amen.

The Unseen Footprints of God

Your path led through the sea,
your way through the mighty waters,
though your footprints were not seen.
You led your people like a flock
by the hand of Moses and Aaron.
PSALM 77:19–20 NIV

In Psalm 77 the psalmist sees the evil happening around him and reassures himself of God's power and control by remembering the mighty things He has done in the past. He thinks of the time God parted the waters of the Red Sea, leading His children to safety on dry ground.

While Moses and Aaron *visibly* led the way, it was really God who led the Israelites, walking before them, showing them the way. His presence left no footprints for the people to see, but He was right there with them.

Remember that. When evil seems to be winning in your world, remember God's power and control. Remember the ways He has worked in your life in the past. Trust that even now He is going before you, preparing the path for you to follow to safety—even though His footprints may remain unseen.

Lord, I know that You always go before. Lead
me along the path You would have me follow,
the path You have prepared for me. Amen.

Nothing

I am convinced that nothing can ever separate us from God's love. Neither death nor life, neither angels nor demons, neither our fears for today nor our worries about tomorrow—not even the powers of hell can separate us from God's love.

ROMANS 8:38 NLT

Is there any promise more beautiful than the one found in Romans 8:38? *Nothing* can ever separate you from the love of God. Nothing you do or say can make God stop loving you. No hidden part of your heart can dissuade Him. Your fears can't chase Him away. Your worries won't change His mind. Even the devil himself can't get in the way of His love for you.

It doesn't always *feel* that way, though, does it? When your heart is aching, when your bank account is beyond empty, when your children are hungry, when you're threatened by others and by doubts in your own heart. But those troubles don't mean you've lost His love. They're just part of living in this fallen world. His love for you has never wavered, not for a moment. Look past the darkness of your troubles and hold tight to the love He's shining into your life. It's yours to keep forever.

Lord, to know that You love me, and to know that nothing will ever stop You from loving me, is a wonderful relief. I rest in Your love, Lord. Amen.

You Need God

*The wages of sin is death, but the gift of God
is eternal life in Christ Jesus our Lord.*

ROMANS 6:23 NKJV

In our DIY society, "I'll do it myself" has become a mantra to live by. But there are some things we just can't do ourselves, like build our own way to God.

You can pressure wash a house, but you'll never be able to wash away your sins through sheer force of will no matter how much pressure you use. You can pry open a paint can or a rusty lock, but you'll never pry open the doors of heaven. You can build a tiny house or even a mansion on earth, but you can't build yourself a home in heaven.

There are some things only God and His grace can do. You need Him. As soon as you accept this and reach out toward Him, He'll wash away your sins, fling wide the doors of heaven, and welcome you into the home He's built just for you.

I need You, Lord, so desperately. And not just for heaven. I need You every moment of every day of my life, and I'm so thankful You are with me. Amen.

But God . . .

> But God raised him from the dead, freeing
> him from the agony of death, because it was
> impossible for death to keep its hold on him.
> ACTS 2:24 NIV

There are times when all seems lost, when nothing but a deus ex machina could save us from our troubles. "But God . . ." may be one of the best phrases in the Bible.

- "*But God* remembered Noah . . ." (Genesis 8:1 NIV; emphasis added here and below).
- "*But God* intended it for good . . ." (Genesis 50:20 NIV).
- "*But God* can be trusted . . ." (Psalm 52:1 CEV).
- "*But God* has blessed you . . ." (Matthew 13:16 CEV).
- "*But God* knows your hearts" (Luke 16:15 NIV).
- "*But God* can do anything" (Mark 10:27 CEV).

Jesus was in the grave, *but God* raised Him up from death. We deserve death, *but God*—through Jesus—paid the price to save us from the grave. Not only did He spare us our punishment, *but God* will also lift us up to heaven to be with Him (Ephesians 2:6).

Lord, so many times throughout my life I know my sins
have earned Your disappointment, even anger. But, God,
You don't turn away from me. Thank You. Amen.

Your First Call

"Call upon Me in the day of trouble;
I will deliver you, and you shall glorify Me."

PSALM 50:15 NKJV

When trouble comes, who do you call for help first? Do you call a family member or a friend? Do you reach out to your church? Do you browse the Internet, looking for someone to call? Or do you just try to work it all out yourself?

It's not that any of these are necessarily bad solutions. But they shouldn't be your *first* one.

When trouble comes, call on God first. Whether you have a broken pipe, a broken bone, or a broken heart, send up a prayer to the One Who is always listening. Ask for guidance, for wisdom, and for rescue. God will answer, and He will deliver you. And when He does, praise Him and tell the world what the Lord has done for you.

Lord, when trouble strikes, my thoughts don't
always go straight to You. Forgive me for that
and help me to call on You first. Amen.

Live in His Peace

God lets you live in peace . . .

PSALM 147:14 CEV

The world can seem like a madhouse these days, and it's not just the wild headlines you see on the evening news or read about on the Internet. The truly unhinged things start to happen when people begin to call good things evil and evil things good. Loving God and using His Word to discern right from wrong is often considered bad. But blaspheming God with words and actions, with greed and hunger for power, is seen as good that should be not just tolerated but encouraged. Crazy, right?

It can be hard to live a Christian life in a crazy world, but you don't have to do it alone. Cast all your anxieties on God (1 Peter 5:7). With God's guidance, even amid the madness of the world, you can live in His peace.

 Lord, when this world turns my world upside down, guide me back to Your perfect peace. Amen.

Unchanging Grace

Jesus Christ is the same yesterday, today, and forever.
HEBREWS 13:8 ERV

O ne of the few things we can be certain of in this world is change. Relationships change, jobs change, your body changes, rules and laws change, and of course the weather changes. Some of those changes can leave you feeling uncertain and wondering who and what you can really count on.

But while everything in this world changes, God never does. He won't change His mind and leave you on your own. He won't change His words to leave you with empty promises. He won't suddenly change the "rules" and leave you outside His grace. People may do those things, but God never will. His love, His promises, and His truth never change. We can count on God, for He is always just the same.

Lord, when this ever-changing world leaves me wondering who I can count on, remind me of the truth that You never change. Your love and guidance and grace are always mine. Thank You, Lord. Amen.

Not One Is Lost

Look up to the skies.
Who created all those stars?
Who created all those "armies" in the sky?
Who knows every star by name?
He is very strong and powerful,
so not one of these stars is lost.

ISAIAH 40:26 ERV

I t's impossible to fully understand the power of God, but if you gaze up at the nighttime sky, you can catch just a glimpse of it. Who created all those stars? Who formed the Bear, Orion, the Pleiades, and all the other constellations (Job 9:9)? Not only did God form all the stars, but He has counted them and knows them so intimately that—just like the sparrows—not one of them is lost without His knowledge.

So when God says that nothing can snatch you out of His hand (John 10:28), that nothing can separate you from His love (Romans 8:38–39), and that nothing could cause Him to lose you (John 18:9), you can know He has the power to keep that promise. Trust Him to hold fast to you today.

Lord, I rest my life, my soul, in Your hands. I trust You never to lose me or let me go. Amen.

Room to Work

Be still before the Lord
and wait patiently for him . . .

PSALM 37:7 NIV

God needs room to work in your life—but how tough is it for Him to find the space?

Our culture puts such a prize on busyness that it's easy for your life to fill up until it overflows completely with appointments with doctors or friends, errands to run, work to complete, and committees to chair. *Could you . . . ? Would you just . . . ? We really need you to . . .* Before you realize what's happened, you're so busy, you barely have time to breathe, much less sit and be still in the presence of God.

Yes, God is with you in all your busyness, but it's in the stillness and quiet that you can hear Him speak to your heart, guide your thoughts, and fill you with His wisdom, power, and peace. Don't fill up every moment with busyness; instead, give your time to God. Give Him room to work in your life today.

*Lord, when I get too busy, remind me to stop, to
be still, and to make room for You. Amen.*

Because

"Forgive us our sins,
as we forgive those who sin against us."

LUKE 11:4 NLT

Why should we love, forgive, and do good to those who ignore us, return our good with contempt, or actively plot against us?

We love, even when we are given every reason not to, because God first loved us (1 John 4:19).

We forgive the wrongs others do us because God forgives the many, many wrongs we do Him.

We do good, even to those who hate us, because God is good to us who hated Him (Luke 6:27).

Who are we to deny others the very gifts of grace, love, mercy, and forgiveness that God has so lavishly given to us? We give to others because so much has been given to us (Luke 12:48).

Holy Father, please forgive me for the times I refused to give to others the very gifts You have so richly given me. Soften my heart and teach me to give the grace I've been given. Amen.

When You Choose Wrong

We know that God causes everything to work together for the good of those who love God and are called according to his purpose for them.

ROMANS 8:28 NLT

You had a decision to make, and you picked the wrong option. Maybe that choice gave you more money, more prestige. Maybe you talked to God about it, or maybe you didn't. Maybe you didn't think about it at all, because it was easier not to. But now here you are, on the other side of that wrong choice, and you're wondering, *Is God done with me now?*

No, of course not! When you make the wrong choice, God doesn't give up on you. He *seeks* you. When you turn back to Him, He guides you back to His side. And in His infinite grace, He uses your wrong choices to teach you, to make you stronger than ever before, and to bring others back to Him. Because God causes everything—even your mistakes—to work together for good.

Lord, forgive me for the wrong choices that I make. Please use me and my mistakes to make Your kingdom grow. Amen.

Stop It

*"Stop judging by the way things look. Be fair
and judge by what is really right."*

<small>JOHN 7:24 ERV</small>

Long hair, short hair, dyed hair, no hair. Tattoos and piercings. Dressed up or dressed down. We find so many ways to judge the way others look and then value their worth based on that. We even find ways to judge the way others worship: singing old hymns or new praises, clapping or not, bowing their heads or raising their hands.

But what did Jesus say about all our judging? *Stop it.* Stop looking at the people around you through the lens of man-made laws and opinions. Instead, choose to see them through the eyes of God's grace—and let's work on those planks in our own eyes instead of the specks in everyone else's (Matthew 7:1–5).

*Father, forgive me for the times I judge others,
especially when I judge them based on things that
don't really even matter. Help me instead to focus
on being the best I can be for You. Amen.*

Victory Today

"Surely God is my salvation;
I will trust and not be afraid.
The Lord, the Lord himself, is my strength and my defense;
he has become my salvation."

ISAIAH 12:2 NIV

What does the word "salvation" mean to you? Does it call to mind images of heaven and angels, a place where there is no more darkness or tears? Do you imagine a place filled with the presence of the Living God? All of these things are true, but salvation is more than just a promised home in heaven someday. Salvation is a promised victory *today*.

Yes, the devil will still attack, and, yes, this world will still throw everything it's got at you. But because Jesus has come, He has overcome this world (John 16:33). Through Him, the victory is already yours. He came so you could have peace and joy—so you could live unafraid—right now. Salvation isn't just for someday. It's for today.

*Lord, I treasure Your promise of heaven someday,
but I praise You now for the salvation You bring
to my life today and every day. Amen.*

"Live" Jesus

Follow God's example, therefore, as dearly loved children
and walk in the way of love, just as Christ loved us and gave
himself up for us as a fragrant offering and sacrifice to God.

EPHESIANS 5:1–2 NIV

If you read through the books of Matthew, Mark, Luke, and John, you'll see that Jesus spoke and healed in the temple and the synagogues (although the Pharisees didn't approve!). But most of His ministry was done outside of those buildings—in the streets, in homes, in gardens, and in nature—amid the day-to-day activities of life.

It isn't what you do behind the closed doors of a church on Sunday morning that brings people to Jesus; it's what you do out in the world on Tuesday mornings and Thursday afternoons, in the lunchrooms, schoolrooms, and boardrooms. It's what you do while you're waiting in line, driving down the road, and just going about the daily business of life. Follow Jesus's example and live like Him in all the moments of your life today, not just the ones inside His church building.

*Lord, teach me to follow Your example,
to live out Your love and grace in all
the moments of my life. Amen.*

Like a Tree

"Blessed *is* the man who trusts in the LORD,
and whose hope is the LORD.
For he shall be like a tree planted by the waters,
Which spreads out its roots by the river . . ."

JEREMIAH 17:7–8 NKJV

How could trusting in the Lord make you like a tree planted by the waters? The answer lies in the next line of that verse: "Which spreads out its roots by the river . . ."

There will be days when your trust in the Lord is well watered by blessings and joys, but there will also be days of drought, when the blessings and joys seem to dry up completely. But when your roots are spread out and sunk deep into the living water of God's truth, you have no reason to fear the heat of drought. Even if it doesn't rain for a year, the leaves of your faith will stay green and tender, encouraging others to believe. When you are like a tree planted by the waters—when you *know* God will do all that He has said He will do—you will be fortified, even on dry days.

*Lord, I thank You for the living water of
Your Word. Teach me to sink the roots of
my faith deep into Your truth, so I can stand
strong in the times of drought. Amen.*

The Power of God

Now may the God of peace . . . equip you with
everything good for doing his will, and may he work
in us what is pleasing to him, through Jesus Christ,
to whom be glory for ever and ever. Amen.

HEBREWS 13:20–21 NIV

"Grace is given not because we have done good works but in order that we may have the power to do them." Augustine wrote these words over 1,500 years ago, but they are no less true today.

God gives you His grace, but it's not because of anything you've done or haven't done. You haven't earned it. It's His gift to you, given out of His great love. But when you accept God's gift of grace, it opens up the power of God to work in your life, enabling you to do all He has called you to do—even those things that seem completely impossible.

Lord, I gratefully accept Your gift of grace.
Pour Your power into my life so that I can do
all that You have called me to do. Amen.

A Song of Grace

The LORD your God in your midst,
the Mighty One, will save;
He will rejoice over you with gladness,
He will quiet *you* with His love,
He will rejoice over you with singing.

ZEPHANIAH 3:17 NKJV

The stories behind songs can be so interesting and unexpected. "Amazing Grace" was written by John Newton, a former slave trader. "Just as I Am" was written by Charlotte Elliott, a chronically ill woman struggling with being confined. Many of David's own psalms were written when he was being pursued by Saul or other enemies.

There's one song whose source of inspiration is completely unique, however. It's the song God sings over you. It has endless variations, one for each of God's children. And while the exact words may differ, it is always a song of His love and delight. It is a song of His grace.

Lord, I pray that my life will give You many
reasons to sing a joyful song. I cannot wait to
one day hear You sing over me. Amen.

You Are What You Wear

*He has dressed me with the clothing of salvation
and draped me in a robe of righteousness.*

ISAIAH 61:10 NLT

When you appear before God, *you are what you wear.* You might have heard this saying before, and it usually has something to do with the latest fashion trends. You aren't better because you wear haute couture or lesser because you wear thrift shop bargains. But when it comes to the way we dress up our own hearts, the saying rings true.

On your own, the best you can hope for is to dress in rags, filthy with sins. But if you bow before Him and choose to follow Him, God gives you a whole new look. He takes those sin-stained rags and tosses them far away, as far as the East is from the West. Then He drapes you in a spotless robe of righteousness, the very one Jesus purchased for you on the cross. Then you truly become what you wear: righteous and saved.

*Holy Lord, I thank You for taking away my sins and
covering me with Your robe of righteousness. It is the
most beautiful garment I will ever wear. Amen.*

Just Like Jesus

*Because of his glory and excellence, he has given us
great and precious promises. These are the promises
that enable you to share his divine nature.*

2 Peter 1:4 NLT

One of the greatest promises that God has given you is that you get to "share in His divine nature." When you love and obey Him with all your heart, soul, mind, and strength, the Holy Spirit of God comes and makes His home inside you (1 Corinthians 3:16). But the Spirit doesn't just live inside you; He gets to work.

Day by day, little by little, the Spirit transforms you from the inside out, making you look more and more like Jesus. The Spirit doesn't give you Jesus's nose or His eyes or the way He walked; rather, the Spirit allows you to live the way Jesus lived and love the way He loved. The Spirit builds up your faith and goodness. He adds to your knowledge and strengthens your self-control. He helps you learn patience and teaches you to be kind to others (2 Peter 1:3–8). As the Spirit works inside you, He makes you holy and divine. He makes you more like Jesus.

*Holy Father, I thank You for Your Spirit inside
me. Please keep working on me, Lord, making
me more and more like Your Son. Amen.*

God's Will

"Thy will be done."
MATTHEW 26:42 KJV

"Thy will be done" is a bit of an intimidating statement. It can be frightening to consider, especially when you think about that night in the Garden of Gethsemane as Jesus prayed desperately. He pled with God to take the cup from Him, yet steadfastly said, "Thy will be done."

God's will for you in your life is being revealed day by day. But whatever the specifics of His will for you are, know that they are governed by this one truth: God's ultimate will is for you to serve His kingdom and live with Him forever. Lift up your prayers to God, lay your requests at His feet, and then submit them to His wisdom with the words "Thy will be done." And trust that God's will for you is always grace . . . because it is.

Holy Father, You know all my hopes and dreams, my wants and needs, but I trust You completely. Thy will be done. Amen.

Let Him Be Your Savior

How often I have wanted to gather your children together as a hen protects her chicks beneath her wings, but you wouldn't let me.

LUKE 13:34 NLT

Have you ever watched a mama bird gather in her chicks? She gently scoops them in with her wings, covers them with her feathers, and stands between them and any coming danger. That's what God longed to do for the people of Jerusalem. That's why He sent Jesus to them. But many of them pushed away His protection and salvation.

Let God gather you in under His wings and cover you with His everlasting grace. Let Him shield you from danger. He sent His Son to watch over you in His love, so don't reject Him. Be vulnerable: Let Him be your Savior today.

Lord, I run to You today. Hide me away from the dangers of this world, safely beneath the shelter of Your wings. Amen.

More Than Just Words

You show love for others by truly helping them,
and not merely by talking about it.

1 JOHN 3:18 CEV

It can be easy to miss the effect you have on the world. Perhaps you think that you aren't really doing that much to make a difference. But when you allow the words of God to prompt you to action, you are doing His will. And that always has an impact.

This world desperately needs to see God—His provision, His protection, His love. And when you give your own lunch to the woman begging at the corner, or when you stop to help the man struggling with his cane up the stairs, or when you share God's story with that person who's so different from you, you are showing the world Who God is. With every word, every smile, every action, you can prove that God is more than just words in an ancient book. You can share His grace.

Lord, I want the world to see how amazing You
are. Give me the opportunity today—and the
courage to seize that opportunity. Amen.

A Chat with God

Because of Christ and our faith in him, we can now come boldly and confidently into God's presence.

EPHESIANS 3:12 NLT

No matter how much you might want to, you can't just march into the White House and have a chat with the president. And you probably won't have an audience with the queen of England anytime soon. Why not? Well, to be blunt, you just aren't that important to them. You don't merit a conversation with these rulers.

But you do merit a conversation with the Ruler of the universe. You can march right into the throne room of God, plop yourself down in front of Him, and have a chat. It can be about the weather, the decision you need to make this week, or the diagnosis that's terrifying you. The God of all creation loves to hear from you, anytime, anywhere, and for any reason. Why? Because He loves you. You are that important to Him. Stop and have a chat with Him today.

Holy Father, I'm so grateful that You love me enough to listen to me anytime, anywhere, and for any reason. Today, I want to talk to You . . . Amen.

The Message of Creation

The heavens proclaim the glory of God.
The skies display his craftsmanship.

PSALM 19:1 NLT

One look up into the sky on a clear night outside the city and it's almost impossible to understand how anyone could question the existence of God. The heavens proclaim and display His handiwork, sending out a message "without a sound or word" (Psalm 19:3 NLT) to declare to all the world that God is real.

Let God's creation speak to you today. See the beauty of the sunrise. Consider how it happens every morning, without fail, and know that you can depend on God. Notice the intricate details of even the tiniest blade of grass or a butterfly's wing, and trust that God cares about the tiniest details of your life. Feel the brush of the wind on your face and know that the Holy Spirit and His love are always with you.

What is God's creation saying to you about Him today?

Holy Father, teach me to see the wonders
of Your creation and to hear what it has
to say about Who You are. Amen.

OCTOBER

Cry Out to God

In my distress I called to the LORD;
I cried to my God for help.
From his temple he heard my voice . . .
He parted the heavens and came down . . .

PSALM 18:6, 9 NIV

S ometimes, when the enemy attacks, crying out to God is all you can do.

The enemy's greatest goal is to separate you from God. He'll attack your work, your relationships, your loved ones, your health, and your wealth. He'll strive to make you feel weak and weary and worthless, to shove you so far down into a pit of worry and fear that you can hardly breathe. And when he does, breathe anyway . . . and cry out to God. Because, yes, sometimes that's all you can do.

But it's always enough.

When you cry out to God, your voice carries all the way to the throne room of heaven, to His very presence. He hears you, and He will part the heavens to come and rescue you.

Lord, today, when the enemy attacks—in big
or small ways—help me remember to cry out
to You. I trust You to rescue me. Amen.

Joy in Heaven

*There will be more rejoicing in heaven over
one sinner who repents than over ninety-nine
righteous persons who do not need to repent.*

LUKE 15:7 NIV

Y ou wandered away from God, but now you've been found,
returned to the fold.

Dear one, don't come back dragging your feet. Don't hang
your head in shame, agonizing over past mistakes. You, sweet
child of God, have been searched for and found by the Lord
God Himself. His grace covers you. He has cast your sins far
away, as far as the East is from the West (Psalm 103:12), and He
remembers them no more (Isaiah 43:25).

Yes, there will be some who are eager to remind you of
the mistakes you've made, even (or perhaps especially) in the
circle of believers. But don't listen to them. Smile, lift up your
head, tilt your ears toward heaven . . . and listen as the angels
celebrate your return!

*Lord, when I—or others—have returned after
wandering away, fill my heart with the joy of
celebration, not the sorrow of guilt. Amen.*

Love Anyway

Even if you suffer for doing what is right,
God will reward you for it.

1 PETER 3:14 NLT

Loving and serving God *anyway*—regardless of the way things are going in your own life—is more than a little countercultural. Our world much prefers to live by standards that help and protect themselves: *Do before it's done to you. Do what makes you happy. Do whatever it takes to make it to the top.*

But *anyway* . . . now, that's a whole different way of approaching life, isn't it? When the job is thankless, serve anyway. When the hurt is deep, forgive anyway. When an enemy's attack was obvious and intentional, pray for them anyway.

We don't love others in a step-on-me, I'm-a-doormat kind of way but in a this-is-what-Jesus-would-do way. Being an example of dedication for all the world to see takes much more courage and strength. Show the world that God loves them as He has loved you—anyway.

Lord, it would be so much easier to just do
what the rest of the world does: to hit back, to
get angry, to turn away. Help me instead to do
what You would do: love anyway. Amen.

Live Anyway

Do not sorrow, for the joy of the Lord is your strength.

NEHEMIAH 8:10 NKJV

This world can really knock you flat with its constant stream of disasters and bad news and negativity. There are horrible things happening in this world, and there are horrible people carrying them out. But if we as Christians go through life with a sour, dour attitude, focusing on girding ourselves up to push through the negativity, who will want to join us?

Enjoy this life God has given you. Delight in His blessings. Savor His creation. Seek reasons to smile and to laugh and to tell others about the wonderful relationship you have with the Lord. Don't let the devil steal away the joy of God's presence and promises that is yours to claim on even the worst of days.

Love God, love others, and love yourself without fear. Trust that the One Who gave you so many reasons to smile will continue to flood your life with His joy.

Lord, open my eyes to see the many reasons I have to smile and praise You this day. Amen.

A Life of Faith

We live by faith, not by sight.

2 CORINTHIANS 5:7 NIV

How do you build a life of faith? Bit by bit, piece by piece, step by step, and day by day.

A faithful life isn't something that suddenly happens all at once, and it isn't something you just stumble into. It takes a lifetime of practice—practicing love, practicing prayer, and practicing mercy and grace.

Such a life is created one memory verse at a time, one Bible study at a time, one prayer at time. Each spiritual practice adds on to the last. It grows as you take first one trusting step, and then the next and the next, following in the footsteps of your Savior. It's built by getting up each day praising God, seeking Him all throughout the day, and then ending your day thanking Him.

Bit by bit, piece by piece, step by step, this journey first begins by accepting God's grace.

Lord, I find myself wishing I could simply have a "ready-made" life of faith. But I know I must build it bit by bit, day by day. Show me today how I can add on to my life of faith. Amen.

A Story of Grace

> My people, listen to my teachings.
> Listen to what I say.
> I will tell you a story.
>
> PSALM 78:1–2 ERV

The Bible is filled with true stories of heroes of the faith who did bold and mighty things, trusting in God to give them the victory. There are also stories of the stumbling and failures of ordinary people who trusted God to bring them back to Him. And, in the grace-filled way of God, these heroes and these failures are often the same exact people. From Adam to Noah, Abraham to Joseph, Rahab to Ruth, David to Mary, and Peter to Paul, their stories teach us how to live a life of faith, covered by the grace of God.

Teach these stories to yourself, to your children, and to their children—all through the generations. Tell them of the God who loves us so much that He sacrificed everything to give us a future with Him. Tell them the story of grace.

Lord, as I pore through Your Word, show me what You would have me to learn this day. Amen.

A Message Worth Repeating

Dear friends, let us love one another, for love comes from God.
Everyone who loves has been born of God and knows God.

1 JOHN 4:7 NIV

Some messages are worth repeating. And when the messages we keep hearing are from God, then it's best to pay close attention to them. One of the messages God repeats over and over again—throughout both the Old and the New Testaments—is love. God Himself is love (1 John 4:8), so if we want to reflect God's image in the way He created us to, we need to be love too. We need to reflect God's own love in every word we say, every thought we think, and every action we take.

This isn't an easy task; in fact, it's probably one of the hardest things God asks us to do. We aren't easy to love. But God demonstrated His perfect love for us by sending Jesus to pay for our sins (1 John 4:10). If we rely on the strength of His love and allow it to fill our hearts with His compassion, we then can live the life of love He has called us to live.

Lord, let my every word, every thought, every
action today, be a reflection of Your love. Amen.

Here I Am

Ananias answered, "Lord, here I am."

ACTS 9:10 CEV

When the Lord called Isaiah, he replied, "Here am I. Send me!" (Isaiah 6:8 NIV). When the angel appeared to Mary, she said, "I am the Lord's servant" (Luke 1:38 NIV), and when God called to Ananias, he said, "Lord, here I am."

None of these people were asked to do easy things. Ananias was told to go and witness to Saul, a man who was terrorizing and hunting down believers. Isaiah was told to be a prophet of God and take His message to a rebellious people. And Mary was told that her life would take a turn into a destiny she could never have planned. Yet each responded with "Lord, here I am"—and their answers still impact our lives today.

When God calls to you today—in something small or something life changing—will you answer, "Lord, here I am"? Because when the tables are turned, when you call on God, His answer is always *Here I am.*

Lord, here I am. Guide me and use me to tell the world—or at least my corner of it today—how wonderful You are. Amen.

They Didn't Know

Jesus said, "Father, forgive them, for they
do not know what they are doing."

LUKE 23:34 NIV

Those soldiers who cast lots for His clothes didn't know. Pilate, who washed his hands of the whole Crucifixion, didn't know. The crowds who mocked and laughed and spat upon Him didn't know. Those Jewish leaders, the very ones who put Him on that cross, didn't fully know what they had done. Even His own disciples didn't truly understand who Jesus was or exactly what He had come to do for them.

But *you* know. You know who Jesus is. You know why He came, why He died, and why He rose to life again. You know that He did all these things to show you His love and His mercy, to give you hope and a future. What will you do today with what you know?

 Lord Jesus, I know who You are: the Son of God who gave up all of heaven to save me. Show me this day what to do with this beautiful truth that I know. Amen.

Disrupted

> The Lord is not slow in keeping his promise, as some
> understand slowness. Instead he is patient with you, not wanting
> anyone to perish, but everyone to come to repentance.
>
> 2 PETER 3:9 NIV

Here's an unsettling truth: God doesn't step into your life to make it all smooth sailing for you. He steps into your life to disrupt it. God wants to rock your world, to shake you up, and force you out of your comfort zone. Would Noah have built that ark, would Esther have left her corner of the palace, or would Peter have left his nets if God hadn't disrupted their lives?

God won't disrupt your life without reason, though. He doesn't want any of His beloved people to perish, and He wants to use you to help Him achieve that goal. His disruption may take the shape of a hurting friend who is finally ready to talk about Jesus—or it may be a life change so massive, you know it can only be His doing. The real question is this: When God disrupts your day, turning it completely on its head, what will you do?

Lord, sometimes I'm afraid I get impatient with
disruptions, even Your disruptions. Open my eyes to see
the opportunities of these disruptions instead. Amen.

Not So Specific

The Lord has told you what is good,
and this is what he requires of you:
to do what is right, to love mercy,
and to walk humbly with your God.

MICAH 6:8 NLT

S ometimes God is very specific in His plans for you. When He gave Noah the plans for the ark, God gave plenty of details, all the way down to the kind of wood to use (Genesis 6:14). When God told Joshua how to knock down the walls of Jericho, there was no question about exactly what he was to do or how many times he should walk around those city walls (Joshua 6). And when He spoke to Ananias, God told him exactly where to go, what to do, and what to say (Acts 9:11).

But more often, God doesn't get so granular. In your daily life, His will may be revealed more by the general guidelines of His Word than by step-by-step, detailed instructions for all the situations of your life. But in all things, you can be guided by Micah 6:8's three tenets: Do what is right, love mercy, and walk humbly with God.

Lord, when Your Word doesn't tell me exactly what
I should do, let me by guided by Your heart. Teach
me to offer love and grace wherever I go. Amen.

He Is Able

Now to him who is able to do immeasurably more than all we ask or imagine, according to his power that is at work within us, to him be glory . . . for ever and ever! Amen.

EPHESIANS 3:20–21 NIV

There is so much we just don't know about God, so much that is impossible for us understand. But we do know that God *does*. He is more than able. He is powerful enough to do infinitely more than we could ever ask or imagine.

God spoke the world—the universe—into existence. He parted a sea to free His people. He enabled ninety-year-old Sarah to give birth to a son. He stilled storms, healed lepers, and raised the dead. By the power of God, sin, death, and the devil were defeated. How exactly did God do all these things? Only He knows that answer. But what we can know is that God will bring that same power that moves mountains to work in your life. Go ahead and ask God to move powerfully in your life today . . . and see how He answers!

Lord, I lay my prayers at Your feet. I trust Your power, and I cannot wait to see how You answer me. Amen.

A Time for Grace

There is a time for everything,
and a season for every activity under the heavens . . .

ECCLESIASTES 3:1 NIV

There is, just as Solomon said, a time for everything. There is a time for you to work and a time for you to rest. A time to laugh and a time to be serious, a time for words and a time for action.

There is also a time to realize you *can't* do it all. There is a time to cook and clean, and a time to just leave it and listen at Jesus's feet (Luke 10:39). There is a time to apologize and a time to stand firm. There is a time to say yes and a time to say no. There is a time to ask forgiveness and a time to forgive yourself. You can't be perfect or make everyone happy. And God doesn't expect it of you. That's why there is also a time to learn to give yourself grace.

Lord, I know that I can't do it all, but it feels
like I should. I know I'm not perfect, but it feels
like I should be. Please help me to understand
that You don't expect these things of me.
Teach me to give myself grace. Amen.

Only God

My God, you are the one who saves me!
Let me sing about all the good things you do for me!

PSALM 51:14 ERV

I t is God—and only God—who saves you.

Not the dream job you dedicated so much time to getting. Not the family you so desperately wanted. Not the friendships or the possessions you cherish. Not the latest or the greatest technologies. And certainly not your own power. None of these things will rescue you in the end; only God can.

It's a humbling thought, to be completely dependent upon His grace. But isn't it also reassuring? All those other things shift and change or even fail. Dream jobs end, families ebb and flow with time and loss, friendships change, and possessions never last. Isn't it such a wonderful relief to know that your eternity doesn't depend on you? God—with His infinite love and unfailing grace—saves you. Sing His praises today.

Lord, let me never get so caught up in taking
my worth from all the things of this world that
I forget You are the One Who saves me. Listen,
Lord, as my heart sings Your praises! Amen.

Someone to Be Praised

Charm is deceitful and beauty is passing,
But a woman who fears the LORD, she shall be praised.

PROVERBS 31:30 NKJV

Proverbs 31:30 reminds us what's really important—not just in a woman but in any person.

People's charm will trick you. It can be put on and taken off again like a mask. And the charm of objects or success just doesn't last. That thing you just had to have often loses its appeal once it's actually yours.

Outward beauty is the same. Appearances—of both people and things—change over time. But the inner beauty of a person who loves the Lord, who worships and reveres Him, who lives life in awe of Him, is something to be praised. Be a person with inner beauty, full of God's love and grace and kindness.

Holy Father, train my eyes to see what
is really important: loving, worshipping,
and living in awe of You. And please train
my heart to do those things. Amen.

What Do You See?

A cheerful heart is good medicine, but a
broken spirit saps a person's strength.

PROVERBS 17:22 NLT

As you get up to start your day, what do you see: all the
things you *have* to do, or all the things you *get* to do? As
you go through your day, do you see all the obstacles in your
path or all the opportunities? And at the end of the day, as you
crawl into bed and reflect, do you see the one thing that went
wrong or the dozens of other things that went so beautifully
right?

Living a joy-filled life doesn't mean you never struggle
with being overwhelmed, never confront obstacles, or never
have anything go wrong. And it doesn't mean turning a naïvely
blind eye to troubles. But it does mean choosing to cheerfully
focus on all that is good and right in your life. It takes practice
and training, but seeing the world through the lens of a cheerful heart can make all the difference in your day.

*Lord, I confess that my cheerfulness could use
a little practice. Teach me to see everything
there is to be cheerful about—starting
with You and Your grace. Amen.*

Be Transformed

Do not be conformed to this world, but be transformed by the renewing of your mind, that you may prove what is that good and acceptable and perfect will of God.

ROMANS 12:2 NKJV

Don't change who you are to fit in with what everyone else is doing. Don't sacrifice what you know is right to avoid the pressure of being different. Because different is exactly what God calls you to be.

God wants you to be *transformed*—different from who you used to be and from the world around you. Let Him change you from the inside out. Dive into His Word, sit at His feet, listen as He speaks, and go where He guides you. As you do these things, and as you spend more time with Him, you will be transformed. He will teach you to want the same things He wants, to see others as He sees them, and to live a life that pleases Him.

Change me, Lord. I place my life, my thoughts, my heart, in Your hands. Make me who You created me to be. Amen.

Pleasing God

Since, then, you have been raised with Christ, set your hearts on things above, where Christ is, seated at the right hand of God. Set your minds on things above, not on earthly things.

COLOSSIANS 3:1–2 NIV

There are a lot of things that can catch your attention in this world. Many of them are good and wonderful, gifts from God. But just as many are distractions. And the devil would love to steal your attention away from anything holy. Greed, lust, anger, gossip—they're the stuff of shallow entertainment. Don't let your focus waver.

When you chose to follow Jesus, you began a new life with Him. The sins of your old life—whatever they were—will try to creep back in. Stop them in their tracks by focusing your attention on Jesus. *Set your heart on things above.* Center your thoughts and actions on those things that are good and pleasing to God, and then *you* will be pleasing God.

Lord, give me the strength to turn away from the sinful things in this world. Teach me to delight in the things that please You. Amen.

Lift and Build

*Encourage one another and build each other
up, just as in fact you are doing.*

1 THESSALONIANS 5:11 NIV

Have you ever seen a video of an old-fashioned barn raising? The entire community gathers together to help. Everyone has a role to fill, from the workers lifting logs to the people offering refreshments and even down to the little ones toting hammers and buckets of nails. Everyone works together to lift up the beams and build the barn.

Building a life in Christ should be exactly like that barn raising. The entire community of believers should gather together to help build each other up in the faith. Everyone has a role to fill, from the workers lifting up those who are hurting, to the ones offering refreshing encouragement to those who are tired, even down to the littlest ones toting smiles and buckets of kind words. As children of God, we are all meant to work together, to build each other up.

What role in the building will you fill today?

*Lord, lead me to that person who needs
encouragement today. May my words and actions
always build up those around me. Amen.*

He Is Coming Back

The day when the Lord comes again will be a
surprise, like a thief who comes at night.

1 THESSALONIANS 5:2 ERV

We don't know the day or the hour, but we know that Jesus is coming back to take His people home. And on that day every knee will bow before Him and every tongue will confess that, yes, He is Lord (Philippians 2:10–11). For the children of God, this will be a wonderful day, filled with unimaginable joy. And the lost will then know how lost they truly are.

Because we don't know when Jesus is returning, we must always be ready. For a child of God, this isn't a reason for fear. Yes, you're still human, which means you're still going to mess up. You're still going to sin. But when you walk with Him, His grace covers you continuously (1 John 1:7). Don't let Jesus's return plant doubt in your heart; instead, let it spur you to action. There's a whole lost world out there that desperately needs Him. Who will you talk to about Jesus today?

Lord, part of me cannot wait for Your return, to see
You face-to-face. But there is part of me that aches
for those who do not know You. Help me to reach
as many of them as I—with You—can. Amen.

The Greatest Help

Friends, please pray for us.
1 Thessalonians 5:25 cev

Whether it's the friend who's hurting right beside us or the missionary in danger half a world away, sometimes we feel helpless. There is so little we can do to aid, to fix, or to make everything good again.

But, oh, how wrong we are! We can offer the greatest help of all: We can pray.

Pray to the All-Knowing One Who gives the perfect answer at the perfect time. Pray to the All-Powerful One Whose might can make everything right again. Pray to the One Who can be where we cannot, Who can strengthen when we cannot, and Who can shield and protect in ways we cannot. First, last, and always . . . pray. It's the greatest help you can give.

Lord, sometimes I find myself saying, "I wish I could do something besides just pray." Forgive me, and remind me that praying is the most helpful thing I can do. Amen.

Protected

The Lord is faithful, and he will strengthen
you and protect you from the evil one.

2 THESSALONIANS 3:3 NIV

There is evil in this world, and, unfortunately, evil is not content to sit idly by. It seeks and searches and prowls like a lion stalking its prey (1 Peter 5:8). And you, dear friend, are the prey.

Yet there is no reason to be afraid. Because the One Who lives in you is greater than all that evil (1 John 4:4). Your Savior has already overcome the world (John 16:33). And though you still live in this world, vulnerable to the evil one's attacks, God does not leave you defenseless. He is your Protector and your Shield (Psalm 28:7).

You may never know—at least, not this side of heaven—all the things God has shielded you from. He may have protected you from physical dangers, spiritual temptations, or relationships that would have pulled you away from Him. The Lord is always working in your life for your good, faithfully shielding and protecting you until the danger is gone, until the day He comes to take you home.

Protect me, Lord, from the evil one and his
traps. Shield me from anything that would
pull me away from You. Amen.

Keep Running

> Let us throw off everything that hinders and the
> sin that so easily entangles. And let us run with
> perseverance the race marked out for us.
>
> HEBREWS 12:1 NIV

Living a life of faith is much like running in a race: not a quick sprint but a marathon. The path is marked out for you, but it's littered with obstacles to avoid, hurdles to overcome, and potholes to dodge. And then there's that adversary in the other lane who keeps trying to trip you up because he just loves to see you fall. It would be easy to simply stay down when you stumble. It would be easy to slide over to the sidelines and sit this one out, perhaps telling yourself that you'll catch up later.

Keep running.

Keep avoiding the temptations, keep overcoming the troubles, keep dodging the sins. And as for that evil one in the other lane, his race has already been run. He loses in the end. But you? Keep running that path with God . . . and you'll win.

*Lord, there are days when it takes all I have just
to stay in the race. Strengthen me, Lord, to keep
running . . . all the way home to You. Amen.*

"Who Do You Say I Am?"

"But what about you?" [Jesus] asked. "Who do you say I am?"
LUKE 9:20 NIV

*W*ho do you say Jesus is?

That's the question Jesus asked His followers all those years ago. It's a good question; in fact, it's *the* question. And it's one He's still asking today.

Was He just a story in a book that's thousands of years old? Was He just a good man or perhaps even a true prophet of God? Or *is* He everything He told us He was: the Messiah (John 4:25–26), the Son of God (Mark 14:61–62). Your answer to that question changes everything. It decides your eternity. So . . . who do you say Jesus is?

*Lord Jesus, I know who You are. You are the
Son of God, my Savior. And I pray that my life
will show the world that I serve You. Amen.*

Faithful

If we are unfaithful,
he remains faithful,
for he cannot deny who he is.

2 TIMOTHY 2:13 NLT

People are changeable. It's not just our appearances that change but also our minds, our hearts, and our actions. And we are unreliable. Sometimes we do what we say we will do, but so often we don't. So often we let the people around us down. We also tend to be inconsistent, saying one thing but then doing another, or downright lying.

People can be faithless, but God is always faithful. God never lies or changes His mind, and He does what He says He will do (Numbers 23:19). Even when we don't keep our promises to Him, He keeps His promises to us (1 Thessalonians 5:24). Because God can't be anything but faithful. It's just who He is—and we should remember to be grateful for it.

Lord, I am so very grateful that You are always faithful in keeping Your promises to me. Forgive me for the times when I fail to do the same. Amen.

Your Inheritance

Now we live with great expectation, and we have a priceless inheritance—an inheritance that is kept in heaven for you, pure and undefiled, beyond the reach of change and decay.

1 PETER 1:3–4 NLT

When you decide to follow God—when you love Him so much that you obey Him—He adopts you into His family and you become His child (Ephesians 1:5). And that's not all: you also become a co-heir with Christ (Romans 8:17) and inherit the glorious riches of salvation (Ephesians 1:18).

These riches can never be stolen from you; they never lose their value, and they are worth infinitely more than diamonds or gold. Your inheritance is the treasure of perfect peace, unending joy, and endless love. It's living for all eternity in a place where there are no tears and there is no darkness, no sadness, no pain. It's walking side by side with the One Who saved you. *That* is your inheritance . . . and it is yours, freely given, because of God's great grace.

Holy Lord, I praise You for the grace that allows me to be part of Your family. And I thank You for the inheritance that You have given me . . . because You love me enough to share eternity with me. Amen.

Great Compassion

Have mercy on me, O God,
because of your unfailing love.
Because of your great compassion,
blot out the stain of my sins.

PSALM 51:1 NLT

Compassion is more than feeling sorry for someone. It's not just understanding someone's pain; it's doing something about it.

God did something about *our* pain. He had "great compassion" on us, His people. God knew we were trapped in our own sins, unable to cleanse ourselves, forever separated from Him—and He did not want to be forever separated from us (Isaiah 43:25). So God did something about it. He sent Jesus, His own Son. Jesus came to take the punishment for our sins, to pay the debt we could never hope to pay (Romans 6:23). And because He did, the stain of our sins is washed away, all because of God's unfailing love and great compassion.

Holy Lord God, I pray You will teach me to show compassion to those around me—to not just see the hurt and the need but to do something about it. Amen.

Saved and Made Whole

"What must I do to be saved?"

ACTS 16:30 NCV

There comes a day in every person's life when we realize that we can't stay hidden—that, yes, in fact, God really does know all those things we've done and said and thought. And, yes, He really will hold us accountable for them. It's then that we have a choice to make: to pretend it doesn't matter, or to fall, trembling, at His feet.

God won't force us to choose Him. If we walk away, He will wait, hopeful for our return. But if we do choose Him, if we put our faith in Him—if we fall to our knees and surrender to Him—He will slip a hand under our chins, He will lift our faces up to His, and with eyes full of love and grace He will heal us, cleanse us, save us, and make us whole in Him.

I choose You, Lord, today and tomorrow and every day. Heal me, cleanse me, save me, and make me whole in You. Amen.

Give Yourself Away

*When He had sent the multitudes away, He went
up on the mountain by Himself to pray. Now
when evening came, He was alone there.*

MATTHEW 14:23 NKJV

D o you ever feel as if everyone wants a piece of you—a piece of your time, your attention, your presence, or your love and care? It's wonderful to be needed and wanted, but sometimes it can be hard to hold yourself together with all those pieces that keep getting pulled away.

But this is the way it's supposed to be, isn't it? Jesus gave His time, attention, presence, love, and care. So, yes, give yourself away. But don't forget to do what Jesus also did: go to God. Let Him give you rest. Let Him renew and restore you. Let Him put all your pieces back together so that you can give yourself away again.

*Piece me back together, Lord.
Make me whole. Amen.*

Carrying the Cross

"Whoever wants to be my disciple must deny themselves
and take up their cross daily and follow me."

LUKE 9:23 NIV

Following Jesus means denying yourself, humbling yourself,
and putting others before yourself. It also means taking up
your cross every day and faithfully carrying it all through the
day—whatever that cross is that God has asked you to bear: a
calling, an illness, or a sorrow.

But there is another cross you should also be carrying: the
cross of Jesus. And while carrying your own cross may sometimes be difficult, carrying the cross of Jesus, with its memory
and promise, is a joyful privilege. It will give you the strength
and courage to carry your own cross, because His cross is your
key to grace.

*Lord, as I go through this day carrying the cross You've
asked me to bear, help me remember the promise of
Jesus's cross and the grace it offers me. Amen.*

Chasing away the Darkness

My God brightens the darkness around me.
PSALM 18:28 NCV

Were you ever afraid of the dark? As a child, you didn't know what the darkness held and you feared the things that might have been in the shadows. As an adult, perhaps you still leave a light on because you do know what the darkness holds: a rug to trip you or a table to stub your toe. You leave a light on so you can see the physical obstacles you need to navigate around.

But there's no lightbulb that can penetrate the darkness of spiritual obstacles, those things in the shadows that try to trip and snag you. Only God can brighten that kind of darkness.

Turn to Him today. Let Him chase away the shadows. That's just what He promises to do: "I am the light of the world. Whoever follows me will never walk in darkness, but will have the light of life" (John 8:12 NIV).

Lord, fill my life with the light of Your truth and love. Brighten the darkness so that I can clearly see how to follow You. Amen.

NOVEMBER

Filled with His Goodness and Grace

Be filled with the Holy Spirit . . .

EPHESIANS 5:18 NLT

Every day is so full of things you need to do and things you want to do, with people and sights and smells and sounds. There are a million and one things that make up a life in this world, and each of those things fills up your time, your thoughts, and your heart.

Today, pour them all out to God and just be empty. Breathe. And then allow Him to pour in His Spirit, strength, love, courage, peace, and joy. Empty yourself of your daily burdens so that you can be filled with the goodness and grace of the Spirit of God.

Lord, I pour out to You all that this world pours into me. Fill me to overflowing with Your Spirit, so that there is only You and none of me. Amen.

It's God's Choice

God said to Moses,
"I will show mercy to anyone I choose, and I will
show compassion to anyone I choose."

ROMANS 9:15 NLT

God chooses who to offer His mercy and compassion to—and, by sending Jesus, He chooses *everyone*. And while it's true that not everyone accepts the gift He offers, it is available to all.

That truth can make us a bit uncomfortable, can't it? It forces us to face our own prejudices and arrogances because we *don't* offer our own mercy and compassion to everyone. But God wants us to.

That homeless woman on the subway who doesn't smell so good, that guy with the tattoos up his arm, and that teenager with the hood pulled up and the pants slouching down—God offers each of them His mercy, compassion, and grace. Your job is to be His hands and His feet, to speak His words in kindness to everyone you come across. Because today and every day God expects you to give the grace you've been given.

*Lord, soften my heart. Forgive me for turning away
from those You would have me turn to. Amen.*

Higher Than the Heavens

Your love reaches higher
than the heavens . . .

PSALM 57:10 CEV

You've heard the saying "I love you to the moon and back again." It's supposed to be the ultimate expression of love—at least, of our human kind of love.

But if you really want to know the ultimate expression of love—to know how great it can be and how far it can truly reach—look to God. "[His] goodness reaches far above the skies" (Psalm 71:19 ERV). His faithfulness touches the clouds (Psalm 108:4). And His love stretches to the moon and beyond, "higher than the heavens," and all the way across the beam of that old wooden cross.

*Lord, I'm not sure I can ever fully understand
the vastness of Your goodness, Your faithfulness,
and Your love. But I praise You and I love You
far more than to the moon and back. Amen.*

Should've, Could've, Would've

He was wounded for our transgressions,
He was bruised for our iniquities;
The chastisement for our peace *was* upon Him,
And by His stripes we are healed.

ISAIAH 53:5 NKJV

"Should've," "could've," and "would've" are often seen as terrible words, filled with lingering regrets for things we wish we'd done and said. They're words that can bog us down in the past and keep us from experiencing the freedom of Christ's great grace.

But what if we saw these words another way: as a reminder to praise God for what He's done for us?

Because it should've been us on that cross so long ago. Jesus could've decided, *No, I won't die a sinner's death. I won't take the penalty for sins I've never committed.* If He had, we would've been doomed to live with our sins forever instead of living with Him.

And here's where the change in thinking begins: Because of grace, it wasn't us on that cross. Jesus didn't say no. And what should've, could've, would've been . . . isn't.

*Thank You, Lord Jesus, that what should've,
could've, would've been isn't so! Amen.*

Does It Matter?

"When you give to the poor, don't let anyone know about
it. Then your gift will be given in secret. Your Father
knows what is done in secret, and he will reward you."

MATTHEW 6:3–4 CEV

Does it really matter if anyone knows you made that donation? Does it really matter if people see your name on that mural you painted for the church nursery? Does it really matter if everyone notices the big bag of groceries you gave to the food room? Does it really matter if anyone sees what a good Christian you are?

The One Who truly matters *does* know. He does see. And not only does God see what you do, He sees why you do it—whether it's for His glory or for your own. If you give, do, and help only to be seen by others, then their praises are your reward. But if you give, do, and help simply because you know it makes God smile, then He rewards you with His heavenly blessings, grace upon grace. And that's what really matters.

Lord, let my gifts always be given for Your glory—
to point others to You and not to me. Amen.

What to Say

> "The Holy Spirit will teach you in that
> very hour what you ought to say."
>
> LUKE 12:12 NKJV

Perhaps it's an opportunity you've been praying to find for so long, or perhaps it's suddenly fallen into your lap, out of the blue. But now you have a chance to tell someone about God, about His great love and the way to heaven. What do you say? What if you say the wrong thing?

Don't let the potential power of that moment frighten you into silence. Remember that God loves that person and cares for their soul far more than you could ever imagine. And remember this beautiful promise: The Holy Spirit—the One God sent to live inside you—will give you the words to say at the moment you need them. Trust Him, turn your heart to Him, and let His words fill your mouth.

Lord, when I don't know what to say, I trust You to give me the words to tell the world—or at least this one person in it—just how wonderful You are. Amen.

Abba

*You did not receive the spirit of bondage again
to fear, but you received the Spirit of adoption
by whom we cry out, "Abba, Father."*

ROMANS 8:15 NKJV

This God you have chosen to follow is the God who created *everything*: every moon, every mountain, every molecule. He is the Lord God Almighty, the One Who holds the key to the storehouses of snow (Job 38:22). He commands the eagles to fly (Job 39:27). The heavens are His throne and the earth is His footstool (Isaiah 66:1).

Who are you to One like Him?

You are His own child. Chosen. Adopted. Dearly loved. And this God who can hold the ocean in His hands invites you to call Him what all children call their fathers: *Abba. Daddy.* That, dear child, is grace.

*Abba, thank You for loving me and
adopting me as Your own child. Amen.*

Every Morning

*Every morning, Lord, I lay my gifts before you
and look to you for help.
And every morning you hear my prayers.*

PSALM 5:3 ERV

Every morning, as you rise, lay yourself before God (physically, if you can), hands and heart open to receive His will.

Lay your will before Him and ask Him to make it match His own. Lay your requests before Him and ask that His will be done. Lay your worries, your fears, your doubts, and all those lingering shadows before Him and entrust them to His care. Entrust *yourself* to His care and lay your gifts before Him. Ask Him to show you how to live and love and serve Him with all He has given you.

Invite—and then allow—God to work in your life every morning and every day, He will.

*Lord, I lay my life before You this morning:
my heart, my mind, my soul, and my strength.
Use me, O Lord, as You will. Amen.*

Begin with God

Lord, show me your right way of living,
and make it easy for me to follow.

Psalm 5:8 erv

Sometimes it's easy to know what to do when things are painted the proverbial black and white, good and bad. Right is clear, and wrong is obvious.

But living in a world full of people, with all their complications and shades of gray, is rarely black-and-white. And that often makes knowing the right choices, the right path, or the right words so difficult. What should you do when it's not clear what you should do?

Begin with God. Ask Him to show you the right way—or just the first step in the right direction. And then remember that God is love (1 John 4:8). Filter every word, every action, and every choice through His love. That doesn't always mean acceptance or even tolerance of just anything. It means loving others enough to reflect God's grace into their lives and to point them ever back to Him. God is love. . . . How are you living His love today?

 Lord, sometimes I know exactly how to show Your love to others, but other times I have no idea what to do. Show me, Lord. Guide me in the right path. Amen.

More Than Just Someone

*Christ's love is greater than anyone can ever know, but
I pray that you will be able to know that love. Then
you can be filled with everything God has for you.*

EPHESIANS 3:19 ERV

Do you ever struggle with the need to prove that you are someone important—someone worthy of attention and of being loved? If so, then you're like pretty much everyone else on this planet.

We get fed a lot of false information about who we are. We're told we should define our worth by numbers on a scale, in a GPA, or in a bank account. But your worth has nothing to do with any of those things. You are worthy because you are a child of God. You are noticed, planned and provided for, and loved by Him.

Don't give anyone or anything the power to define your worth except God. Because you are more than just *someone* to God; you are *everything* to Him (Isaiah 43:25).

*Help me, Lord, to look to You to know who I am
and what I am worth. Remind me that I am Your
child and anything else is just extra. Amen.*

Live the Sermon

*Now when Jesus saw the crowds, he went up
on a mountainside and sat down. His disciples
came to him, and he began to teach them.*

MATTHEW 5:1–2 NIV

It's called the Sermon on the Mount, and it's found in Matthew 5–7. It won't take you long to read through it, but these teachings of Jesus touch on how to live every part of your life for God. They aren't complicated, but they can be difficult to accomplish—a narrow path to follow.

That is why you must ask God to help you. Seek His wisdom and His will. Keep knocking on the door of heaven with your prayers. He will answer (John 15:7), He will be found (Jeremiah 29:13), and He will show you the way (Proverbs 3:5–6).

Seek to live the sermon in your life as best you can with His help and His strength.

*Lord, guide me in living out Your words.
Help me never to stray from Your side. I give
You my life, my praise, my all. Amen.*

Healing Leads to Serving

Jesus went into Peter's house and saw his mother-in-law lying in bed with a fever. So he touched her hand, and the fever left her. Then she got up and began to serve him.

MATTHEW 8:14–15 CSB

Jesus healed Peter's mother-in-law. In this same chapter, Matthew 8, He also healed a leper and a centurion's servant, cast out demons, and stilled a storm. But what Jesus really does in this chapter is give us a glimpse of His Father—the One Who touches the untouchable, the One Who heals with a word, and the One Who has authority over storms and evil. God is so loving that He chose to take the punishment for our sins, and He is so great that He was able to do it.

Notice that after she was healed, Peter's mother-in-law got up and began to serve Him. And that is our example to follow. By His wounds we are healed (Isaiah 53:5), and because we are healed, we should get up and serve Him.

Just as grace received leads to grace given, healing leads to serving.

 Lord, You have healed me completely and eternally. Please guide me to serve You completely and eternally. Amen.

Impossible Reality

"With God all things are possible."
MATTHEW 19:26 NKJV

Jesus came and did what could not be done by man. He didn't merely make the impossible possible; Jesus made it a reality. He carried out physical and spiritual impossibilities: He healed and raised the dead to life, and He overturned the Pharisees' laws and traditions with grace.

Why? Because Jesus had compassion. He saw with His own eyes, heard with His own ears, felt with His own heart, and touched with His own hands. And if you let Him, He'll transform your impossibilities into reality—like the impossibility of a sin-free life transformed into the reality of God's welcoming arms.

Lord, I praise You for making the impossibility of heaven a reality for me. Amen.

Jesus Knew

> It was just before the Passover Festival. Jesus knew
> that the hour had come for him to leave this world
> and go to the Father. Having loved his own who
> were in the world, he loved them to the end.

JOHN 13:1 NIV

Jesus knew everything that was coming that night: the prayers, the garden, the arrest, and the trial. He knew everything that would come the next day too. He knew He would die.

And yet He chose to spend those last moments with His friends. He chose to praise God and break bread with them. And in kneeling to wash their feet—even the feet of one who would soon prove to be His enemy—He chose to teach them one last time.

What does that tell you about how much Jesus valued His friends that He chose to spend some of the last moments of His life with them? When you obey Jesus, He calls you friend (John 15:14), and He chooses to spend every moment—into eternity—with you.

Lord Jesus, I thank You for the indescribable gift of Your friendship. There is no relationship more precious to me. Amen.

Asking

I will answer their prayers
before they finish praying.
ISAIAH 65:24 CEV

Asking for help isn't always easy. Perhaps that's because asking is a way of admitting your own weakness, showing that you need someone else's help to accomplish what you need to do. And then, of course, when you ask someone to do something for you, there's always the risk that they will say no.

Could those be the same reasons you don't always ask God for what you need? Do you not want to admit to Him you can't do it alone or that you need help to do what must be done? Could it be you're afraid that He will say no, so rather than take that risk, you just charge ahead on your own?

Don't be afraid to admit you need God. And don't be afraid that he will say no to you: It's a given that he will protect you. Ask for His help, and know that as soon as you start praying, His answer starts coming.

Holy Father, forgive me for the times I barge
ahead on my own without seeking Your guidance
and help. I know I need You to lead me. Amen.

Longing for Home

> We are citizens of heaven, where the Lord Jesus Christ lives.
> And we are eagerly waiting for him to return as our Savior.
>
> PHILIPPIANS 3:20 NLT

Do you ever find yourself longing for home like Dorothy from *The Wizard of Oz* even as you stand in the middle of your own home?

You feel it like a distant memory deep in your heart: You *know* there is better place, a world without all the struggle, or the sadness, or the temptation. You know that somewhere there must be a home where you can truly rest and truly be safe.

You feel that way because, as a child of God, this broken world in its current state is not your home. And all these struggles are "light and momentary troubles" that will achieve for you "an eternal glory that far outweighs them all" (2 Corinthians 4:17 NIV). Hold on. Jesus is coming back, and He will make a home for you.

Holy Father, I thank You for the promise of an eternal home. As I live in this world, I pray that You would help me to live in a way that shows others where my true home is. Amen.

Present in the Silence

Everyone, be silent!
The LORD is present . . .
ZECHARIAH 2:13 CEV

S ilence can be uncomfortable for us. We live in such a noisy world that when we find ourselves in moments of silence, we struggle to fill it. In those moments at the hospital, at the graveside, or in the face of loss, we sometimes fill the silence with a rush and tumble of words that may be better left unsaid. And in our moments with God we do the same: We fill the silence with a flurry of requests, a repetition of words that quickly become meaningless.

Sometimes what is really needed is simply to be present in the silence.

Don't be afraid of the silence. Let your presence—your smile, your hug, your shared tears—speak for you in those moments when you have no idea what to say. And in those moments with God, do the same. Let your presence—your seeking, searching, submitting-to-His-will presence—tell Him all He wants to hear.

Lord, I come to You now and I wait in silence before You. . . . Amen.

Watched

*On a Sabbath day, Jesus went to the home of
a leading Pharisee to eat with him. The people
there were all watching him very closely.*

LUKE 14:1 ERV

The people were watching Jesus very closely, but not just to see what He did and certainly not to learn from Him. They were watching to see if He would make a mistake. They were waiting for Jesus to mess up.

Do you ever feel that people are watching you, just waiting for you to mess up so they can trap you and make you feel small or stupid? Maybe it's a micromanaging boss or a family member or friend who loves to be critical. Maybe you even feel like God is watching you, waiting to point a finger and shout "Aha!" when you make a mistake. (He isn't, by the way.)

When you mess up—and we all do—take hope in this truth: Jesus didn't make a mistake that day or any day. He *never* messed up. He came and lived a perfect life so that you don't have to.

*Holy Father, I am so grateful that You are a
God who doesn't watch me, waiting for me to
make a mistake. Instead, You watch over me,
waiting to pick me up. Thank You. Amen.*

All She Had

A poor widow came and put in two very small
copper coins, worth only a few cents.

MARK 12:42 NIV

Her story takes up only a few lines in the Bible. We don't really know much about her, we don't even know her name. But the few things we do know about her speak volumes.

She is "a poor widow." These words whisper of loss and mourning and a broken heart. There is the hint of hunger and a struggle to survive. But we don't really feel pity for her, do we? She is so *fiercely* faithful. She could have made so many excuses: not to be there, not to give. But she didn't. She was there at the temple. She saw the rich giving out of their wealth. And rather than shy away in shame, she gave "everything—all she had to live on" (Mark 12:44 NIV). She had faith that God would provide for her. She might have been a poor widow, but she was rich in the things that matter most. Are you?

Lord, help me to give all I have—heart, mind,
body, and soul—to You. I want to be rich
in the things that matter most. Amen.

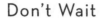

Don't Wait

*"Then he said, 'I know what I will do. I will tear
down my barns and build bigger barns!'"*
LUKE 12:18 ERV

Jesus told the story of a man so rich, his barns would not
hold all his crops. So he decided to tear them all down
and build bigger ones in order to keep everything he owned
for himself. But that night he died, and all those things he had
hoarded meant nothing.

This story reminds us to share our possessions, the physical
objects that we cannot take with us. But what if you applied
that story to your heart as well?

Are you being selfish with other things besides *things*? Are
you withholding friendship because you don't want to invest the
effort? Are you withholding talents out of fear? Are you withholding service because of a reluctance to give up your free time?
Are you withholding your praises and your deepest self from God?

Every moment is precious, but every moment is not promised. Don't wait to share yourself and your gifts with God and
those around you. What can you share today?

*Lord, forgive me for the times I withhold
myself from the world and even from You.
Please give me the courage and the will to give
my heart freely, especially to You. Amen.*

How Wide?

I pray that you and all God's holy people will have the power to understand the greatness of Christ's love—how wide, how long, how high, and how deep that love is.

EPHESIANS 3:18 ERV

You know God loves you, but do you know just how strong His love for you truly is?

God's love for you—for each and every one of His children—is unimaginably great. It reaches higher than the heights of the heavens and deeper than the oceans He scooped out with His own hands. It is unending, lasting longer than time itself. But the width of God's love for you is only a few feet wide—just the span of an old, rugged cross on the hill of Calvary.

And that is something to be thankful for today and every day of the year.

Lord, I don't believe that I can ever truly understand how much You love me, at least not this side of heaven. But I am so grateful You choose to love me. Amen.

Do More

If anyone has material possessions and sees a
brother or sister in need but has no pity on them,
how can the love of God be in that person?

1 JOHN 3:17 NIV

We often tell each other that we should count our blessings, and this is a wonderful and necessary thing to do. But, starting now, do more: For each blessing you count, challenge yourself to *be* that blessing to someone else.

Thank God for the blessing of your family, and then invite someone who has no family to share in your own. Thank God for the blessing of friends, and then be a friend to someone who is alone. Thank God for the blessings of food and clothes and shelter, and then do what you can to help the ones who lack those.

This Thanksgiving season, and all through the year, count your blessings . . . and then do more.

Lord, I praise You for all You have given
me. Please show me how I can use those
blessings to bless those around me. Amen.

Give Your Heart

"What sorrow awaits you Pharisees! For you are careful to
tithe even the tiniest income from your herb gardens, but
you ignore justice and the love of God. You should tithe,
yes, but do not neglect the more important things."

LUKE 11:42 NLT

Jesus didn't criticize the Pharisees because of what they gave
to others; rather, He criticized them for what they didn't give.

The Pharisees were very careful to give a tenth of everything
they produced, even down to the tiniest herbs they grew in their
gardens. But they didn't give the more important things, like justice to their fellow man. Often they were so intent on following
the letter of God's laws and their own man-made traditions that
they didn't follow the more important heart of God's laws: love.

Do you ever find yourself being a bit of a Pharisee? Do
you ever give just enough to check off a box on some imagi-
nary list so that you can be a "good Christian" while ignoring
what you know in your heart God wants you to do?

When you give, yes, give your money and your possessions. But also give your heart. Because God gave you His . . .
and He never stopped to count the cost.

*Holy Father, forgive me for the times when I try
to please You by just "checking off a box." Help
me to give without counting the cost. Amen.*

The Way Jesus Gave

"When you give a dinner or a supper, do not ask your
friends, your brothers, your relatives, nor rich neighbors,
lest they also invite you back, and you be repaid."

LUKE 14:12 NKJV

D o you only give to those who can give something back to
you? We like to give when we know we'll see results, but
try something different today. Give to someone who can't give
back or who won't be grateful. Give when you won't be around
to see it make a difference.

Your heavenly Father will see what you do, and He'll
know why you do it (Matthew 6:4). And when you give to
honor God, you'll be blessed by knowing you've done as Jesus
did on the cross. You'll have given to someone who can never
repay you, who will never give as much as you've given, and
who often forgets to even say thank you. Give the way Jesus
gave to you.

*Holy Father, place opportunities in my path
today to give to someone, to help someone with
no expectation of even a thank-you. Amen.*

Everything You Could Ever Want

I went to your temple,
and there I understood
what will happen
to my enemies.

PSALM 73:17 CEV

When you look around in the world today, it seems like evil triumphs and the good guys finish last. There's nothing new to this feeling. The psalms are filled with David's complaints about the wicked prospering. Read through Psalm 73 and see if you haven't encountered some of these same types of people in your own life: the arrogant, the selfish, and the downright cruel.

Then read Psalm 73:17: "I went to your temple, and there I understood what will happen to my enemies." Although the wicked may seem to win, God sees the evil they do, and they are in great danger of losing everything that really matters (Psalm 73:18–20). Yes, you still have to deal with these kinds of people, but remember as David did: God holds your hand. By His grace, He leads you and guides you all the way home to Him. And God is everything you could ever want (Psalm 73:23–25).

Holy Father, please give me the words to tell the
world how wonderful You are—so that maybe the
wicked will choose not to be wicked anymore. Amen.

Faithfully Forgiven

*If we confess our sins, He is faithful and just to forgive
us* our *sins and to cleanse us from all unrighteousness.*

1 JOHN 1:9 NKJV

Y ou were right there, teetering on the edge, about to fall
into sin (Psalm 73:2). But you didn't. You wised up. You
listened to the warnings to God and His Word. You stepped
back from the edge and away from sin, and you praised God for
helping you to stand strong.

Or maybe you didn't. Maybe you were teetering on the
edge and then fell into that sin. You didn't wise up or heed the
warnings. Instead of stepping back, you dove right in. Now
the reality of what you did has begun to sink in. Now what?

Go to God. Tell Him what you did and that you know
how wrong you were. And then praise Him for the faithfulness
of His forgiveness that He promises is yours.

*I praise You, Lord, for the times You've helped me
stand strong against sin and for the times You've
forgiven me when I've fallen yet again. Amen.*

God Alone

Great is the LORD and most worthy of praise;
his greatness no one can fathom.

PSALM 145:3 NIV

We can measure the height of the mountains, the volume of water in the oceans, and the distance to the sun and the moon. But no one can measure the greatness of our God.

God controls day and night, winds and snows and seasons (Psalm 74:16–17). God created amoebas and antelopes, molecules and man. His power is simply too great for us to understand.

And God pours that same power into your life. He will lift you up when you've fallen (Psalm 145:14) and rescue you when you call Him (Psalm 145:19). He is always righteous and kind. God alone is worthy of your praise, because God alone "always keeps his promises" and "is gracious in all he does" (Psalm 145:13 NLT).

You alone, Lord, are worthy of my praise. So to
You alone I give my life, my love, my all. Amen.

Never Too Far

If I rise on the wings of the dawn,
if I settle on the far side of the sea,
even there your hand will guide me,
your right hand will hold me fast.

PSALM 139:9–10 NIV

You are never too far away for the grace of God to reach you. If you travel to a foreign land, God can still guide you home, even if you fled into your own sins. Just ask that prodigal son. If you run away to hide in the belly of a ship and then find yourself in the belly of a whale, God can still hear and answer your prayers. Just ask Jonah. Not even the tomb can separate God from the ones He loves and the ones who love Him. Just ask Jesus.

No matter how far from God you wander away—or even run away—you're never so far that His hand can't reach you, never so far that His love can't hold you, and never so far that His grace can't forgive you.

Thank You, Holy Lord, for holding fast to me.
Please strengthen my hold on You. Amen.

Two Goals

He who is in you is greater than he who is in the world.

1 JOHN 4:4 NKJV

The devil has one goal: to pull you away from God. He does it with tricks and traps that make good seem evil and evil seem good. He does it with whispered lies like *Who do you think you are?* and *You're not fooling anyone. Everyone knows what kind of person you really are.* And he does it with guilt and shame: *You've already messed everything up* or *What's the point in trying to be good now?* or *Not even God could forgive that.*

God has one goal too: to pull you closer to Him so close that you become the temple His Spirit lives within. He never tricks or traps or lies. He offers you the pure truth of His Word, limitless love, and unending grace. And He really hopes you'll choose Him.

There are two completely opposite goals: one pure goodness and one pure evil, one of God and one of the devil. Guess who's stronger? Choose God.

I choose You, Lord. Today and every day of my life, I choose You! Amen.

It Is I

"It is I. Don't be afraid."
MARK 6:50 NIV

The day had been spent teaching and then feeding thousands. Jesus was tired, and He needed to be alone with His Father. So He sent His disciples ahead of Him in the boat, saying He would meet them in Bethsaida. Then He went up on the mountainside to pray. Meanwhile, the wind was against the disciples, and they strained against the oars without success. Then they saw Jesus.

When Jesus said He would meet them at Bethsaida, the disciples surely thought He meant to get another boat or perhaps walk around the Sea of Galilee to get there. They never expected to see Him walking across the waters. But that's exactly what He did.

Jesus often works in quiet ways, but sometimes He appears in your life in big, bold, walking-on-the-water ways. Don't be afraid. Welcome Him into the boat of your life and let Him guide you safely through the waters.

*Lord, don't let my fear of the unexpected
keep me from seeing You. Amen.*

DECEMBER

The Gift of Presence

I keep my eyes always on the LORD.
PSALM 16:8 NIV

It's so easy to get lost in the going, the giving, and the doing of this season. December rushes in on the tail of Thanksgiving in a whirl of things to do, places to be, and expectations to meet. And then you blink, and January is knocking upon the door. And you wonder, *Did I celebrate Christmas? Did I enjoy my loved ones? Did I rejoice in my Savior at all?*

People will tell you to slow down and cut back, but chances are you can't eliminate all the busyness. What if, instead, you decided to simply *savor* it—to see not all the endless "have-to-dos" but rather all the wonderful "get-to-dos"? This season, determine to seek the joy of Jesus in all you do. Be fully present in each moment this Christmas. It's a gift you can give yourself, your loved ones, and your Savior each day of this wonderful season.

 Lord, help me to be present in all that I do this season, to savor each moment, and to seek Your presence. Amen.

Set Christ Free

*So whether you eat or drink, or whatever
you do, do it all for the glory of God.*

1 CORINTHIANS 10:31 NLT

Christmas has been kidnapped. A sacred celebration has been hijacked by commercialism, held hostage with ropes of busyness, and tied up with a big red bow of holiday expectations. Set Christmas free this year. No, don't give up on the decorating, the giving, the gathering, but rather:

- Decorate your home with the beauty of the season, and as you do, pray that God will decorate your heart with the beauty of His Spirit.
- As you wrap each gift, pray that God will wrap each person in His love and care.
- Gather with those you love and invite God to gather with you.

Let Christ's love shine through you amid all the busyness of the season. Because He is the greatest gift you can give.

*Lord, it's so easy to lose sight of the reason for
the celebration while we're celebrating. Remind
me that Christmas is for You. Amen.*

The Sparrows

"What is the price of five sparrows—two copper coins?
Yet God does not forget a single one of them."
LUKE 12:6 NLT

Imagine a God so immense and so powerful that He spoke the universe into existence—an ever-expanding universe so huge that we can only guess at its vastness. Now imagine that same God so intimately involved in His creation that He knows the fate of every tiny common sparrow.

God spoke His creation into existence, from the heavens to the waters, from the mountains to the sparrows (Genesis 1). But you? God made you from the dust, breathing His life into you. God knit you together in your mother's womb, lovingly and thoughtfully creating you with His own hands (Psalm 139:13). If God knows the fate of all those little sparrows He spoke into being, how much more does He know and love and care for you, the one He created with His own hands? Whatever comes your way today, for good or for ill, know that your Father in heaven is watching over you in deep, unchanging love.

Lord, it is impossible for me to fully understand
who You are and all that You have done. And how
amazing it is that not only do You notice me but
You know me and love me. Thank You! Amen.

The Light of the Word

*"I am the light of the world. Whoever follows me will
never walk in darkness, but will have the light of life."*

JOHN 8:12 NIV

Light is an amazing thing. It cuts through the darkness and
sends the shadows scurrying away. How many childhood
fears were banished with a simple beam of light?

But the light of Jesus is more than beams that shine out
from the sun or wavelengths from a lamp. The light of Jesus is
the truth, pure and without a speck of darkness in it. It cuts
through the lies and nonsense of this world and sends the devil
scurrying away.

As you walk through the holiday season with all its beautiful lights, let each one remind you of Jesus and His truth.
Praise Him for the light He brings to your world.

*Lord, let me never take the light You shine into
this world and into my life for granted. Amen.*

The Only Judgment

There is therefore now no condemnation to those
who are in Christ Jesus, who do not walk according
to the flesh, but according to the Spirit.

ROMANS 8:1 NKJV

There's no shortage of people willing to judge us in this
world. We may have bosses who say we're not sharp
enough for the promotion, teams that say we're not good
enough to play with them, friends who decide we're too needy,
or spouses who decide we aren't worth being married to—even
fellow Christians who tell us that we're too messed up for God
and His grace.

The thing is the judgments of those people don't add up to
a proverbial hill of beans. Only God's judgment matters. And
when you invite Him into your life—when you choose to follow Him and commit to obeying His will over your own—then
the only judgment you receive from Him is this: *Not guilty by
reason of My grace.*

*Lord, there's so much You could choose to condemn me
for. Thank You for giving me grace instead. Amen.*

Jesus Is . . .

For to us a child is born,
to us a son is given,
and the government will be on his shoulders.
And he will be called
Wonderful Counselor, Mighty God,
Everlasting Father, Prince of Peace.
ISAIAH 9:6 NIV

Jesus is so much more than the greeting-card, only-in-December Savior we have too often made Him out to be.

Jesus is . . . the child born in a Bethlehem stable more than two thousand years ago. He is the Son of God, sent to earth to live as a man. He is the Wonderful Counselor who comes to comfort us in our grief (2 Corinthians 1:3–4). He is One with the Mighty God, One with the Father (John 10:30). He is unchanging and eternal (Hebrews 13:8).

Jesus is not only the King of kings and Lord of lords; He is also the Healer and Forgiver and Source of Joy. Jesus is unfailingly and radically kind *to us*. For the One Who so long ago reached out to touch the untouchables is still reaching out today to lift up all those who have been cast aside. To lift up *you*. Because Jesus is . . . grace.

Lord Jesus, when I am asked who You are,
I say that You are everything! Amen.

The Joy of the Spirit

Jesus was filled with the joy of the Holy Spirit, and he said,
"O Father, Lord of heaven and earth, thank you . . ."

LUKE 10:21 NLT

Jesus praised God because He was filled with the joy of the Holy Spirit. And because Jesus came, you can be too.

Allow yourself to experience the joy of the Spirit today. Put down the phone, turn away from the screen, and take note of the blessings God has lovingly and thoughtfully placed all along your path. Pause and really look at the wonders of His creation. Enjoy the loved ones in your life. Savor time in His Word. Sit with Him and feel His Spirit working within you, guiding your heart to sing His praises. And, as Jesus does in Luke 10, thank your Father for the things He has hidden and the things He has revealed.

Still me, Lord. In the rush of this day, fill
me with the joy of Your Spirit. Amen.

Be Happy

"Be happy that your names are written in heaven!"
LUKE 10:20 CEV

Take a moment to think about what makes you happy. What makes you smile? Maybe it's the joy of friendships you can count on, having someone who loves you to share your smiles with. Or maybe it's the sharp, clean smell of snow as it whispers to the ground, or the welcome warmth of a steaming mug of hot cocoa on a brisk winter's day.

God has given us so many wonderful things in this world to make us happy, to make us smile. And we should enjoy these things, because they're God's gifts to us (James 1:17). But there is one thing that should make you happier than any other thing, and it is this: As a child of God, your name is written in heaven with the ink of grace.

 Thank You, Lord, for the many things You've given me to make me smile. Thank You most of all, though, for the grace that writes my name in heaven. Amen.

So Be It

All honor and glory to God forever and ever! He is the eternal
King, the unseen one who never dies; he alone is God. Amen.

1 TIMOTHY 1:17 NLT

When it comes at the end of a prayer, "Amen" means "so be it." Paul often used the word at the end of his praises to God: "To him be glory for ever and ever. Amen" (2 Timothy 4:18 NIV). He also used it at the end of his blessings to others: "The grace of our Lord Jesus Christ be with your spirit, brothers and sisters. Amen" (Galatians 6:18 NIV). And, of course, it is found at the end of prayers: "May the God of peace . . . work in us what is pleasing to him, through Jesus Christ, to whom be glory for ever and ever. Amen" (Hebrews 13:20–21 NIV).

"Amen" agrees with whatever was stated before it; more than that, it asks God to carry these things out. As you say your own praises, blessings, and prayers, deliberately end them in "Amen" and then pause for a moment to consider the meaning it adds. *Lord, You are mighty. So be it. . . . May God bless you today. So be it. . . . Your will be done. So be it, Lord.*

 Holy Father, I praise You, I humble myself *before You, and I pray that Your will be* *done in every part of my life. So be it.*

A New Way

For I am about to do something new.
See, I have already begun! Do you not see it?
I will make a pathway through the wilderness.
I will create rivers in the dry wasteland.

ISAIAH 43:19 NLT

There's no way out. You've calculated and recalculated, and there's just no way to pay all the bills this month. You've apologized and begged for forgiveness, but you can't seem to fix that relationship you hold so dear. You've tried every solution you can think of, but that problem just won't go away. Don't give up. Don't despair. Give your troubles to God.

God has a way of untangling the fiercest of knots when you give them to Him. That's the key, though. God won't jump in, snatch your troubles away, and then hand them back again, all fixed. But when you call on Him to work in your life and in your struggles, God will be there. When you can't see a way out, He'll make a new way for you, a pathway through the wilderness of your troubles and rivers of peace in the midst of your storms.

Lord, please work in my life. Show me the way—the new way—You would have me follow You. Amen.

One Day at a Time

*"Do not worry about tomorrow, for
tomorrow will worry about itself."*

MATTHEW 6:34 NIV

There's an old joke that asks: "How do you eat an elephant?" The answer is: "One bite at a time." Whenever you tackle any project—whether it's building a house, going back to school, or walking a faithful life with God—if you only look at how huge the gap is from where you are now to where you want to end up, you'll be overwhelmed.

So don't try to eat the whole elephant; just take the first bite. Pick up the phone, pick up the books, and pick up your feet to step out in faithful obedience to God today . . . and then tomorrow . . . and then the next day. One day at a time, live and love and walk beside your Lord. He'll be there every step to strengthen and encourage and cheer you on all the way to your journey's end.

*Holy Father, it's tempting to look at the
whole of my journey, with all its struggles and
challenges, and be overwhelmed. Remind me
that a faithful life is really just living one day
at a time with You by my side. Amen.*

Coming Soon

After Noah was 500 years old, he became the
father of Shem, Ham and Japheth. . . .
Noah was six hundred years old when the
floodwaters came on the earth.

GENESIS 5:32, 7:6 NIV

I t's easy to lose our sense of timing when we read through the
account of Noah and that ark he built. These few verses only
take us moments to read, but they took Noah decades to live out.

While scholars disagree about exactly when Noah started
building the ark, we know the flood didn't begin until decades
later, when Noah was six hundred years old. Why did God
wait?

The answer is simple: *grace*. Noah surely wasn't silent all
those years in the midst of all that evil. He was telling everyone
who would listen and everyone who laughed that the Lord's
judgment was coming. This was their chance to turn to Him.

Are we using these precious years before the Lord's return
to tell the people He is coming soon? That this year, this season, this day, is their chance to turn to Him? Today, think of
ways that God can use you to speak His love to others.

*Lord, I praise You for Your patience. Please give me the
words and the courage to tell all who will listen—and even
those who will laugh—that You are coming soon. Amen.*

The Gift Within You

Do not neglect the gift that is in you . . .
1 TIMOTHY 4:14 NKJV

God has given you a gift that's unlike the gifts He's given to anyone else in the world. It may not be painting the ceiling of the Sistine Chapel. It may not be composing a hymn of hallelujahs to Christ the King. It may not even be volunteering in the nursery on Sunday mornings. But you can be sure that it's there, ready for you to use it for Him.

While others may have similar gifts, there's no one in the world who can use that gift in quite the same time, place, and way that you can. So don't neglect it. Don't leave it unused or hidden away. Whether it's painting or composing, teaching preschool or cooking, preaching or encouraging, use the gift God has given you today.

Lord, forgive me for the times I don't have the courage—or simply don't take the time—to use the gift that You've given me. Teach me how best to use my gift to praise You. Amen.

Every Good Gift

*Every good and perfect gift is from above, coming
down from the Father of the heavenly lights,
who does not change like shifting shadows.*

JAMES 1:17 NIV

Take a moment to consider all the good things in your life. From home and food to family and friends to the worldly riches of cars and jobs and bank accounts, each of these can be a gift from God.

But God doesn't only gift us with the things of this world. Some of His most precious gifts are the ones that only our hearts can see. Think about that word of encouragement when you needed it most, that whispered verse from His Word that gave you just the answer you needed, or simply the power of His presence when you're feeling lost and alone. These aren't random happenings or coincidence. Every good and perfect thing in your life is a *thoughtful* and *intentional* gift from God. And the greatest of these gifts is His love poured out in the sacrifice of His own Son . . . for you.

*Lord, open my eyes today to see all the gifts
You've given me—and help me remember to
thank You for each and every one. Amen.*

So You Could Be Rich

You know the generous grace of our Lord Jesus Christ.
Though he was rich, yet for your sakes he became poor,
so that by his poverty he could make you rich.

2 CORINTHIANS 8:9 NLT

When you think of riches, what comes to mind? Perhaps it's the luxuries of this world: money or jewels, mansions or yachts. But what price would you pay for unending peace, immeasurable joy, and limitless love? Those are the true riches: the heavenly ones. And those are the very things Christ chose to leave behind when He stepped down from heaven and into the dust of that Bethlehem manger.

Jesus left the peace of heaven to live amid the strife of men. He left immeasurable joy to weep with the ones He loved. And He gave up limitless love in exchange for bitterness and hate. Jesus left behind all the riches of heaven. Why? *For your sake.* For your sake, Christ became poor . . . so that He could give you all the riches of His grace.

Lord Jesus, I cannot imagine leaving behind
all the riches of heaven . . . but You did it to
save me. And I praise You, with all my heart,
for giving those riches to me. Amen.

Not So Little

Clothe Yourselves with . . . kindness . . .
COLOSSIANS 3:12 NIV

It's the little things that can mean the most: that smile you offer the lady in line behind you with the fidgety toddler; that extra big tip for the waiter who's so obviously having a really rough day; that "How are you?" that isn't just polite but says, *Yes, I really do want to know how you are.*

When small kindnesses become a routine part of your day, they can make a huge impact on the world around you. Because little things aren't so little when they're done through the love of Jesus. Leave a trail of little kindnesses behind you wherever you go . . . a trail that others can follow right to the heart of God.

Lord, open my eyes to see the little things I can do to brighten another's day today—and all the million little things You do for me. Amen.

A Genealogy of Grace

This is the genealogy of Jesus the Messiah the son of David, the son of Abraham . . .

<small>MATTHEW 1:1 NIV</small>

Take a moment to read Matthew 1:1–17. Don't let your eyes simply gloss over all those names as we so often do. Read them slowly. Note each person. Remember their stories. Some are better-known than others. Some we don't know at all. But note the ones you do know.

There's a liar named Abraham and a cheat named Jacob. Rahab the harlot is followed by Ruth the heathen. David is there despite the adultery and murder. Solomon is there too with his wealth and splendor and idolatrous ways. There are kings, good and bad and terrible. All those names lead to Jesus.

Don't think you have to be perfect to be part of Jesus's family tree, because the genealogy of Jesus is a genealogy of grace.

Holy Lord, thank You for making me part of Your family tree. Amen.

Finding Favor with God

Then the angel said to her, "Do not be afraid,
Mary, for you have found favor with God."

LUKE 1:30 NKJV

Mary found favor with God, but she wasn't perfect. She was good and kind and faithful but not perfect. And isn't that part of what makes her story so wonderful? God didn't require Mary to be perfect in order to receive His favor or to find her place to serve in His kingdom. And He doesn't require *us* to be perfect, either.

God could choose to look at our imperfections and hold them up as a reason not to use us in His work. *Liar. Doubter. Gossip. Sinner.* But He doesn't. In fact, God in His infinite grace sent His Son to offer us His own robe of righteousness to cover over our imperfections (Isaiah 61:10). Because it isn't perfection that finds favor with God; it's a heart that is willing to serve.

*Lord, Mary's answer to You was "I am the Lord's
servant" (Luke 1:38 NIV). Please fill me with
Your courage and strength so that will be my
answer today and every day of my life. Amen.*

Joseph

*When Joseph woke up, he did as the angel of the
Lord commanded and took Mary as his wife.*

MATTHEW 1:24 NLT

Joseph doesn't get a lot of attention in our Christmas narratives. He's the one dutifully leading the donkey in the children's book illustrations. He's the robed figure quietly standing in the background while the shepherds gather round. He's that largely invisible figure patiently teaching Jesus the craft of working with wood.

And yet Joseph is key.

Joseph obeys the angel without question and takes Mary as his wife—and then likely listens to a lifetime of whispers about their Son. Joseph's hands deliver the King in that Bethlehem stable. Joseph rises in the night and leads them to safety. Joseph, most likely, teaches his Son how to be a craftsman.

Your role in God's kingdom may or may not get a lot of attention. At times it may be dutifully quiet, even largely invisible. But never doubt: You are key to Him.

*Holy Father, help me to serve and to obey You
without question, whether it's serving quietly and
invisibly or for all the world to see. Amen.*

Pondering

*Mary treasured up all these things and
pondered them in her heart.*

LUKE 2:19 NIV

Mary had seen some amazing things—an angel, the Son of God in the form of a baby, shepherds rushing to kneel and to praise—and she knew these were not ordinary things. So she kept them. She treasured them all up and *pondered them in her heart.*

We don't do enough pondering these days. Perhaps it's because, in the hustle and bustle of this world, there is so much vying for our attention. But you too have seen some amazing things. Think about them now: those things that took your breath away and those things that left you knowing without a doubt you had been in the presence of God. Keep those things close. Treasure them all up and ponder them in your heart.

*Lord, there are times when I have felt Your
power and seen Your majesty. Teach me to notice
those times, to remember them, and to ponder
the wonder of You and Your grace. Amen.*

The Reason

Christ Jesus came into the world to save sinners . . .
1 TIMOTHY 1:15 NKJV

A stable was certainly not where you would expect the King of all kings to be found. It was dusty, smelling of hay and animals. There was no crown for His head, no throne for a seat. A roughened manger that once held food for the animals now held the Light of the world. And as humble as this stable was, the reason He came was even more humbling.

Jesus came to grow up here on earth, experiencing all the joys and heartaches we do. He came to endure all the same trials and temptations we do. He came to teach us about the Father—*His* Father—and show us how to love. And He came to be punished for our sins so He could save us.

Lord Jesus, You endured so much to save me. Help me to live this day in thanks to You for all You've done for me. Amen.

The Shepherds

*There were shepherds living out in the fields nearby,
keeping watch over their flocks at night.*

LUKE 2:8 NIV

Imagine being one of those shepherds out in the fields that night—a night like any other—watching over the sheep, perhaps gathering around a campfire, laughing and talking with your fellow watchers. And suddenly a flash of light, a sky transformed by the glory of the Lord, and an angel proclaims the most wondrous news: The Messiah is born! The armies of heaven fill the air with their presence and praises . . . and then all is still again.

But the shepherds aren't still. They are running to Bethlehem, to Mary and Joseph, to the baby in the manger. They are kneeling before Him in awe and wonder, and they are telling everyone they meet about what they have seen.

Why shouldn't we do the same? In the busyness of this season, make time to run to Jesus, to kneel before Him in awe and wonder, and to tell everyone about the One you have seen.

*Holy Lord Jesus, I run to You now, I kneel here at
Your feet, and I offer You all my praises. Amen.*

Like a Star in the Sky

*You will shine among them like stars in the sky
as you hold firmly to the word of life.*

PHILIPPIANS 2:15–16 NIV

The wise men traveled from a far-off land to see Him, following the star that lit their way all the way to the King. It took years, and when they finally found Him, they fell to their knees and worshipped Him (Matthew 2:1–12).

There is no star in our night sky that leads people to Jesus—but God has placed you in the lives of others. You can lead those who seek Him through the darkness of this world all the way to the King. With your words that echo His Word, with hands that serve, with feet that go where you are needed—and, most all of all, with a heart that loves as He does—you can shine like a star in the sky. You can light the way and lead others to Jesus.

*Lord, I thank You for all those who have shone
in my life, leading me to You. Help me to be
that same light for others to follow. Amen.*

DECEMBER 24

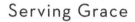

Serving Grace

"Even the Son of Man came not to be served but to serve
others and to give his life as a ransom for many."

MATTHEW 20:28 NLT

Jesus could have come to earth with all the might and power of heaven's armies behind Him—but He didn't. He could have come bearing all the riches of the storehouses of heaven—but He didn't. He could have come as the King of all kings—but He didn't do that, either.

Instead, Jesus came as a baby in a borrowed manger, the Son of a poor carpenter and his wife.

He didn't come to conquer armies, live in luxury, or rule the nations. He came to lift a woman out of the dirt, to weep with friends, and to wash His betrayer's feet.

Service was Jesus's gift of grace to us, and it's a gift you can give others. How can you use it to bless others today?

*Lord Jesus, You came to serve; it was Your gift to us.
Show me how I can serve someone today. Amen.*

When Grace Came Down

She brought forth her firstborn Son, and wrapped
Him in swaddling cloths, and laid Him in a manger,
because there was no room for them in the inn.

LUKE 2:7 NKJV

I s there a day that changed your life? Perhaps it was the day you got the job, the day you got married, or the day a child was born. Or maybe it was the day of the big storm or the big move. The events of one day can change your entire world.

But there was one day that changed the whole world. It was the day that God became man—the day Jesus took His first step out of heaven and His first step toward the cross. That day changed not just the whole world but the whole of eternity. On the day our Savior was born, grace came down from heaven to us.

Lord Jesus, You left all the perfection of heaven
to come to this dusty, dirty, sin-filled world . . . to
save me. I can never thank You enough. Amen.

DECEMBER 26

A Part of the Path

"The Son of Man must suffer many terrible things," he
said. "He will be rejected by the elders, the leading priests,
and the teachers of religious law. He will be killed, but
on the third day he will be raised from the dead."

LUKE 9:22 NLT

As terrible and senseless as Jesus's suffering on earth was,
it wasn't without purpose. With that suffering came a
promise. Yes, there would be rejection. Yes, there would be
persecution. And, yes, there would be death. But there would
also be resurrection. Jesus would suffer and die, but then He
would be raised to new life.

And you, dear friend, have exactly that same promise. Yes,
there will be suffering in your life. And although we would all
rather skip that part of the promise, that suffering is a part of the
path that leads to salvation. And it's that side of the promise—a
new life in heaven—that helps us endure the suffering and even
find joy within it (James 1:2–4). Keep your eyes on God and find
joy today in the promise of a new life in heaven.

 *Holy Father, it's so easy for me to allow troubles and
difficult times to pull my eyes and my heart away from
You. Help me, Lord, to hold tight to You and to Your
promise of a new life, free from all suffering. Amen.*

In the Home of God

Lord, who may dwell in your sacred tent?
Who may live on your holy mountain?
The one whose walk is blameless,
who does what is righteous,
who speaks the truth from their heart . . .

PSALM 15:1–2 NIV

Could there be any better place to be than in the home of God? In his psalm, David asks what kind of person could hope to dwell in God's sacred tent. The answer can be troubling: "The one whose walk is blameless, who does what is righteous, who speaks the truth from their heart." Who could possibly meet those requirements? Who would dare to call themselves blameless?

On our own, none of us—not even the best of us—could claim to be blameless or righteous. But we are not on our own. Jesus walks with us, covering all our faults and sins with His perfect grace so that we can appear blameless and righteous before God. And if we follow Him, Jesus has prepared a place for us in the house of God (John 14:2–3).

 Lord, like David, my greatest prayer is to live forever in the sacred tent of Your home—and to help as many people as possible to join me there. Amen.

Where Do You Look for Help?

God, my strength, I look to you for help.

PSALM 59:9 ERV

When you need help with problems big or small, where do you look? Do you rely on your own strength to see you through? Do you turn to friends for advice? Do you look to your family to support you? Do you wander the aisles of the bookstore, thumbing through self-help books?

None of these answers are wrong, but they aren't the best answers, and they shouldn't be your first answers. Turn to God's Word, His strength, and His guidance. He is the One Who loves you perfectly and has endless resources to help you. So when you're looking for help—or even if you aren't—run to Him first.

Lord, You are the shelter I can always run to, the strength to see me through. I will sing Your praises for all to hear. Amen.

Keep the Peace

*If it is possible, as far as it depends on you,
live at peace with everyone.*

ROMANS 12:18 NIV

It's always a bit surprising to discover how vicious and vengeful some people can be. A quick read through David's psalms will tell you, though, that this is nothing new. Some people enjoy stirring up trouble. Don't be one of them. And when you get caught in the trouble they've stirred up, don't pay back evil for evil (Romans 12:17). Don't seek revenge (Romans 12:19). Instead, do your best to keep the peace, if it is possible.

If it is possible . . . which means, of course, that sometimes it isn't. Some people aren't content to leave you in peace—and that's when it's time to leave *them* in peace. Walk away. Quit the scene. It takes two people to argue, so remove yourself from the equation. Instead, repay their evil with the goodness of your prayers and leave the rest to God. Trust Him to see that justice is done.

*Lord, there are those who seem to enjoy causing trouble.
I pray that You would change their hearts—and
until then I pray that You would shield me from their
attacks. Help me to return their evil with good. Amen.*

Making Plans

We can make our plans,
but the Lord determines our steps.

PROVERBS 16:9 NLT

You've got a plan. You've thought it through and laid it out step by step. All you need to do is follow it, and it will lead you straight to your goal.

Except that it doesn't.

You had it all figured out. What could have gone wrong? Why didn't your plan—for your life, your job, your family, or even just your day—work out? Because it was *your* plan, not God's.

We have a funny way of thinking we're in control of our lives. And while we can choose our actions and our reactions, it's God's plan for our lives that reigns supreme. It's His will that *will* be done. If He says *No* or *Not now,* then at some point your plan will fail. God isn't being cruel and He isn't being heartless. He's protecting you from things that would harm you and He's guiding you toward something much better than what you have planned. He's showing you His grace.

Lord, I entrust my plans for today to You. I trust You to guide me in the way I should go—even if Your plans are different from mine. Amen.

A New Beginning

If anyone is in Christ, he is a new creation; old things have passed away; behold, all things have become new.

2 CORINTHIANS 5:17 NKJV

When you decide to live your life for Jesus, you become a whole new creation. Oh, you may look the same on the outside. But inside—in that eternal part of you that is your soul—you are made completely new. Every sin is erased, and you can be sure that God will never again hold them against you.

As a new creation, you'll also learn to see the world and the people around you in a whole new way. Your focus will shift from yourself to others as you see things through the eyes of God's love and Jesus's sacrifice. You'll be given a new, tender heart (Ezekiel 36:26).

As you anticipate this new year, take time to examine the mistakes, the missteps, and the sins of the past year. Learn from them. Vow not to repeat them. Then put them behind you and step into the new beginning of this new year—holding fast to God's hand and to His grace.

"Create in me a clean heart, O God, / And renew a steadfast spirit within me" (Psalm 51:10 NKJV). *Amen.*

NOTES

These pages have been provided for your personal journaling and meditation.

Notes

....
....
....
....
....
....
....
....
....
....
....
....
....
....
....
....
....
....
....
....
....
....
....
....

Notes

Notes

Notes

Notes